Military Recruiting Outlook

Recent Trends in Enlistment Propensity and Conversion of Potential Enlisted Supply

Bruce R. Orvis

Narayan Sastry

Laurie L. McDonald

Prepared for the
United States Army
Office of the Secretary of Defense

RAND

The research described in this report was sponsored by the United States Army under Contract No. DASW01-96-C-0004 and by the Office of the Secretary of Defense (OSD) under RAND's National Defense Research Institute, a federally funded research and development center supported by the OSD, the Joint Staff, and the defense agencies, Contract No. DASW01-95-C-0059/TO01.

Library of Congress Cataloging-in-Publication Data

Orvis, Bruce R.
  Military recruiting outlook: recent trends in enlistment
propensity and conversion of potential enlisted supply / Bruce R.
Orvis, Narayan Sastry, Laurie L. McDonald.
      p.   cm
  "Prepared for the United States Army and the Office of the
Secretary of Defense."
  "MR-677-A/OSD"
  Includes bibliographical references. (p.   )
  ISBN 0-8330-2461-2 (alk. paper)
  1. United States—Armed Forces—Recruiting, enlistment, etc.
2. Soldiers—Supply and demand—United States. 3. High school
students—United States—Attitudes. I. Sastry, Narayan.
II. McDonald, Laurie L., 1955-   .   III. United States. Army.
IV. United States. Dept. of Defense.   Office of the Secretary of
Defense. V. Title.
UB323.0784   1996
355.2'23'0973—dc21   96-48738
                                                                CIP

RAND is a nonprofit institution that helps improve public policy through research and analysis. RAND's publications do not necessarily reflect the opinions or policies of its research sponsors.

Published 1996 by RAND
1700 Main Street, P.O. Box 2138, Santa Monica, CA 90407-2138
1333 H St., N.W., Washington, D.C. 20005-4792
RAND URL: http://www.rand.org/
To order RAND documents or to obtain additional information,
contact Distribution Services: Telephone: (310) 451-7002;
Fax: (310) 451-6915; Internet: order@rand.org

Based on RAND's past body of recruiting research and on indications of increased difficulty in meeting recruiting goals, in spring 1994 the Army Chief of Staff and the Deputy Secretary of Defense asked RAND to examine recent trends in the recruiting market and their implications for meeting accession requirements. The request for assistance consisted of two parts: (1) a quick initial examination of the trends and (2) a longer-term research agenda to study the recruiting outlook in depth. The results of the preliminary examination were briefed in May 1994 and are documented in RAND report MR-549-A/OSD, *Recent Recruiting Trends and Their Implications: Preliminary Analysis and Recommendations.* This report presents results from the longer-term analysis. Its findings should be of interest to planners and policymakers concerned with recruiting.

The research is continuing. We are in the process of updating our econometric models of enlisted supply, and seek to identify both economic and attitudinal enlistment motivators for subgroups of the youth population, including women and different race-ethnic groups. Our analysis of supply conversion also continues. This includes estimating the effects of demand-side factors and analyzing recruiter stationing data to help determine how changes in stationing and recruiting practices may have affected recruiting success.

The research is being conducted within the Manpower and Training Program, part of RAND's Arroyo Center, and within the Forces and Resources Policy Center, part of RAND's National Defense Research Institute. The Arroyo Center and the National Defense Research Institute are both federally funded research and development centers, the first sponsored by the United States Army and the second by the Office of the Secretary of Defense, the Joint Staff, and the defense agencies.

CONTENTS

FIGURES

TABLES

SUMMARY

RAND first reported its project findings on recruiting trends in spring 1994. We found that the supply of potential enlistees exceeded its predrawdown level relative to the accession requirement. We argued that reported problems in meeting monthly recruiting goals could be due to difficulties in converting potential supply into enlistment contracts. Such difficulties could arise from changes in the attitudes of society and key influencers—such as parents, friends, and school counselors—that could affect the advice given to youth about the desirability of joining the military or the access given to recruiters to talk to youth about enlisting. Also, possible drawdown-related changes in resource allocation and management could hinder conversion. Such changes could include, for example, the allocation of resources for different modes of advertising; different recruiter stationing practices; or changes in the goals given to recruiters and the incentives provided to meet those goals.

Although we argued that conversion issues were likely to explain the reported difficulties and that they needed resolution, we also worried about DoD's ability to meet the increased postdrawdown accession requirement. Consequently, we argued for a hedging strategy that included increased advertising and relief from the congressionally mandated ceiling on the number of recruiters. We focused on these resources because of their demonstrated cost-effectiveness and flexibility.

Our strategy also included a reexamination of the enlisted supply results and an in-depth examination of conversion issues, the subject of this report. We begin by examining the possibility that the models on which the initial results were based might have overpredicted supply to a degree sufficient to have masked actual shortages. This seems unlikely, given the level of supply predicted and the consistency of the results generated by the propensity (attitudinal) and econometric models we used, which employ very different techniques and variables. Below we summarize the updated propensity analysis. The econometric analysis is ongoing and will be reported on in a separate document.

SUPPLY OF POTENTIAL ENLISTEES

In analyzing potential supply, we reestimated the relationship between the stated intentions of survey respondents and their actual enlistment decisions, which was originally quantified by RAND in the 1980s. The reanalysis corroborates the findings of the earlier research. Intentions stated in the YATS still predict enlistments; moreover, the rates of enlistment for different intention groups are consistent with those derived in the earlier analysis. Analysis of recent trends in propensity for high-quality male youth reaffirms that predicted supply for FY94 and FY95 generally exceeded its FY89 level relative to accession requirements. In other words, if anything, the supply of potential high-quality enlistees had generally increased since the beginning of the drawdown—when recruiting was good—relative to the accession requirement. Thus, the recent difficulties reported by recruiters in FY94 and FY95 came at a time when potential supply appears to have been adequate; this suggests problems in converting supply into enlistments.

Notwithstanding the results for FY94–95, there has been some downturn in youth interest in military service. When that downturn is coupled with the large postdrawdown increase in accession requirements for the Army and Marine Corps, we find that the potential supply of high-quality enlistees could fall short of its predrawdown levels. Thus, by FY97 we may have to overcome a supply problem in addition to conversion issues. The downward trend is greater for high-quality minority youth, particularly African-Americans, whose propensity has fallen far more steeply than that of other race and ethnic groups. This raises additional concerns about the military's ability to continue to achieve the level of social representation that it has today.

CONVERSION OF POTENTIAL SUPPLY

Although the data show reductions in the rate at which potential high-quality recruits discuss military service with key influencers such as family members and friends, the magnitudes of the reductions are consistent with the general reduction in propensity. That is, the size of the predicted decrease in enlisted supply is similar for the two indicators. Thus, these reductions do not appear to constitute an additional problem. Still, we might worry if the advice received by youth who do have such discussions had become more negative. While the results are not conclusive, we found no evidence that the counsel provided by parents or friends has become more negative over the past several years. Similarly, results from DoD's Recruiter Surveys suggest that the advice given to students by school counselors concerning military service has remained constant during this period.

A related issue involves access to high school students. As we indicated earlier, had there been a downturn in societal or influencer favorability toward the military, we might have expected some potential increase in the difficulty of gaining access to students in high school. As just noted, however, we found no evidence of such a downturn in attitudes. Similarly, we found little change in recruiters' ability to gain access to high schools. According to the Recruiter Surveys, recruiters, if anything, report increased visits to local high schools. Moreover, there is virtually no change in recruiters' reported ability to gain access to high schools to talk to seniors about enlisting, display their materials, give talks in classes, or be present at career days. Similarly, results from the Military Entrance Processing Command (MEPCOM) database on high school Armed Services Vocational Aptitude Battery (ASVAB) administrations suggest no decline in recruiters' access to students and test results over the past several years.

Although gaining access to high schools does not appear to have become more difficult, other data suggest nonetheless that there has been some decline in the rate of contacts between recruiters and high school students. While the rate of contact has, if anything, increased slightly for high-quality high school graduates, a downturn in high school contacts with prospective high-quality recruits is reflected by reports from current students about contacts with recruiters during the last twelve months. The reduced level of contact is consistent with lower propensity, but the fact that it is concentrated among high school students suggests the importance of other factors.

One reason for reduced contact could involve reductions in the numbers of recruiters and stations made during the drawdown, which could have made some markets more remote and reduced the feasibility of maintaining predrawdown visitation levels. A second factor could involve episodic shifts in the recruiting focus to high school graduates rather than students, in order to meet short-term shipping goals during times of increased recruiting difficulty. An additional possibility involves the downturn in the rate of high school ASVAB administrations—revealed by MEPCOM records for both the number of schools testing and the number of students tested per school—which are known to be a good source of leads. This reduction could result from reduced recruiter presence at high schools, or it could be contributing to the reduced level of contacts with high school students.

RECOMMENDATIONS

We find the total pattern of results to be consistent with declining propensity plus continuing difficulties in converting potential supply into enlistments. The conversion problems may result from a variety of factors; as noted, one of these is possible isolation from some markets. Based on these results, our interim recommendation is to consider increases in advertising, educational benefits, and the number of recruiters; this should ensure that the DoD will meet current recruiting goals and be positioned to meet the increased accession requirements in FY97. It is important to act soon, considering the proximity of the increase and the lead time required to put the resources in place. The recommended resources have been shown to be the most cost-effective resources for recruiting high-quality youth. Moreover, they are flexible: They can be increased or decreased as needed.

To further enhance cost-effectiveness and because demand-side practices such as resource allocation decisions and goaling are important determinants of recruiting success, we also recommend that decisions about resource increases be preceded by identification of specific shortages that need to be remedied. For example, are shortages concentrated in specific types of jobs, or are they endemic in many specialties? This has implications for targeting and cost. Similarly, are the shortages concentrated in specialties with limited benefits, or are they present in specialties that already offer maximum benefits? In the latter case, the implication could be to increase the maximum value of the benefit; in the former, it would suggest increasing the number of specialties offering the maximum current benefit. Similar arguments can be made with respect to other options, for example, different terms of service. The basic question is how the presence or absence of shortages in occupational specialties covaries with the options that are available. These patterns should be reviewed to obtain guidance on the types of actions and magnitudes of incentives that may be used to improve the recruiting picture cost-effectively. By analogy, a similar strategy should be considered with respect to possible increases in recruiters and stations. The question here becomes whether recruiting shortages are more pronounced in markets that have become more isolated or have experienced larger reductions in the recruiting force, or whether they are prevalent throughout the country. The answer to this question provides guidance on the desired number of recruiters, stations, and locations.

ACKNOWLEDGMENTS

We would like to express our gratitude to Lieutenant General Theodore Stroup, Major General Thomas Sikora, and Major Leonard Wong (then) of the Office of the Army Deputy Chief of Staff for Personnel, and to Dr. W. S. Sellman and Major Dana Born of OSD's Accession Policy Directorate, our sponsors. We also are grateful to the Defense Manpower Data Center and, in particular, to Dr. Jerome Lehnus, Mrs. Randolph Lougee, and Mr. Thomas Ulrich for their continued support in providing data and analysis for this research, and to Dr. Veronica Nieva and Dr. Michael Wilson of Westat. Thanks are due also to the U.S. Army Recruiting Command and to the Military Entrance Processing Command for their cooperation in providing recruiting information. We also would like to express our gratitude to Lieutenant Colonel James Thomas, for his help while in ODCSPER and later during his year as an Army fellow at RAND, and to our RAND colleagues Peter Tiemeyer and Bryan Hallmark, for their thoughtful reviews, Nikki Shacklett, who edited and helped in preparing this report, and Fran Teague, for her skill and patience in finalizing it.

Chapter One

INTRODUCTION

BACKGROUND

Since the late 1980s, the military has been successful in recruiting high-quality youth into the all-volunteer force. But by 1994, concerns about the future prompted the Office of the Secretary of Defense (OSD) and the Army to ask RAND to assess recent recruiting trends and their implications for meeting accession requirements. Successful recruiting, like successful marketing of any kind, requires an adequate level of resources. By fiscal year 1994, very substantial cuts had been made in those resources as part of the post–Cold War military drawdown. For example, the number of Army recruiters had been cut by 25% since 1989, and advertising cuts exceeded 50%. Moreover, in FY94 the military faced the prospect of continuing cuts in those resources, due to congressionally mandated ceilings on the number of recruiters and other budgetary constraints. At the same time, a downturn in youth interest in joining the military had been reported and widely noted. That report seemed to be confirmed by indications from recruiters of more difficulty in meeting their monthly goals.

Either of these occurrences would have caused concern in its own right; they took on added significance in the context of the post-drawdown increase in the annual military accession requirement. During the drawdown, accessions—the number of youth brought into the military each year—were deliberately cut below the level needed to sustain the force. This avoided having to induce even more people to leave the military who otherwise might want to stay. Now that the drawdown is ending, annual accessions have to be re-

1

stored to the level needed for sustainment. This involves a substantial increase.

As shown in Figure 1, records from the Office of Accession Policy in OSD indicate that annual accessions of non-prior-service youth into the military were reduced by about 100,000 during the drawdown, from approximately 275,000 in FY89—the last predrawdown year—to approximately 175,000 in FY94, when they bottomed out. Then accessions began to increase. The increase in FY95 was small; by FY97, however, the planned increase becomes substantial, amounting to 18% across the Department of Defense (Air Force, Army, Marine Corps, Navy) according to the services' FY1996–2001 Program Objective Memorandum (POM) projections (i.e., their budget submissions to DoD). The prospective increases vary by service; for the Army, which had the biggest drawdown, the increase is about 45% relative to FY94.

ENLISTMENT PROCESS

Figure 2 provides a conceptual overview of the enlistment process. It illustrates how the factors we discuss in this report relate to enlistment and to each other. The process can be visualized in two stages: initial propensity formation, i.e., establishment of potential supply, and conversion of that potential supply into enlistments. Figure 2 illustrates the basic propensity-conversion-enlistment relationship. That is, if propensity decreases, the number of enlistments would be expected to decrease (if the conversion rate did not increase). If enlistments decrease, the cause could be a decrease in propensity or conversion or both.

"Propensity" can be thought of as an overall measure that summarizes the influence of a variety of factors on youth's initial interest in joining the military. This includes the attitudes of key influencers (such as parents and friends), youth labor market conditions, and recruiting resource levels and allocation. On the basis of past RAND research, we know that there is a strong relationship between youth's stated propensity to join the military in surveys and their actual eventual enlistment decisions (Orvis et al., 1992). Similarly, we also know that there is a strong relationship between youth labor market conditions (e.g., youth unemployment levels) or recruiting resource

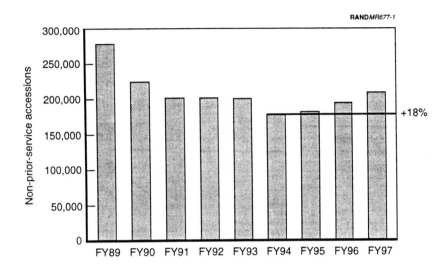

Figure 1—Annual Recruiting Requirements

levels (e.g., advertising budget or number of recruiters) and enlistment rates. (See, for example, Cotterman (1986), Dertouzos et al. (1989), Fernandez (1982), Hosek and Peterson (1985), and Polich, Dertouzos, and Press (1986).)

The above factors relate to potential supply. Past research shows that there is also an important conversion process that determines how much of the potential supply is actually captured (in the form of enlistment contracts). (See, for example, Asch and Karoly (1993), Asch (1990), Berryman, Bell, and Lisowski (1983), Daula and Smith (1986), Dertouzos (1985), and Orvis, Gahart, and Schutz (1990).) Conversion may be affected by the views of society and key influencers toward the military. These views affect the counsel youth receive from their family, friends, and school advisers as they reach a final decision about joining the military, and they also may affect the access of recruiters to youth in school (or at home) to discuss enlistment. Past work also shows the importance of recruiter and resource management factors in the conversion of potential supply, for example, the enlistment contract goals given to recruiters and the incentives provided to achieve those goals. Such factors also would include the ways available resources are allocated, for example, the mix

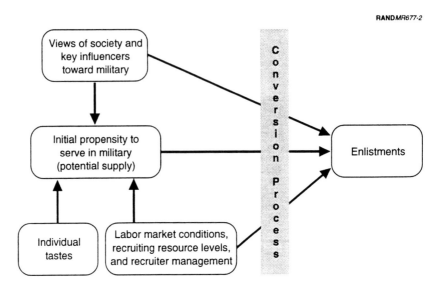

Figure 2—Conceptual View of the Enlistment Process

of media used in advertising or the number and location of recruiting stations.[1]

KEY FINDINGS OF THE INITIAL EXAMINATION

To provide a point of departure for the results presented in this report, we now review the key findings of our initial examination of recent recruiting trends. (The results of that effort were reported in Asch and Orvis (1994).) At that time, we found that the potential supply of enlistees relative to the FY94 accession requirement exceeded predrawdown levels. This conclusion was reached independently by both a propensity analysis and an econometric analysis, even though they employed very different methodologies and vari-

---

[1]Additional arrows and/or boxes could be added to Figure 2. For example, the demand for enlistment contracts affects the actual number of enlistments, recruiting resource levels, recruiter management, and in the case of pay changes, labor market conditions. In turn, recruiting resource levels and their management and youth labor market conditions can affect the views of society and key influencers toward military service.

ables. In the case of propensity, we found that the decline for the prime recruiting market through fall 1993 was not large and should not have caused supply problems. Similarly, in the econometric analysis we found that although there had been substantial cuts in recruiting resources during this period (that should have adversely affected recruiting), their effects had been outweighed by changes in the youth labor market favorable to recruiting, for example, a large increase in the youth unemployment rate. (See Asch and Orvis (1994), p. 25. The econometric analysis is now being revised, with attention to changes in coefficients over time and to trends specific to women and minorities.)

Given these findings, what could the reported recruiting difficulties be attributable to? We saw two possible explanations. The first—but in our view the less probable—was that the true supply level[2] was below that predicted by the models used in the propensity and econometric analyses. We did not attach much credence to this explanation because the models had been developed over a period of many years in many different recruiting environments and political climates; we believe they should be robust against possible changes in recruiting due to the end of the Cold War and the drawdown. Moreover, the results of the two models were strong in their implications and were consistent not only with each other but with those of other econometric models we examined. Nonetheless, we recognized that our longer-term research should update the models and use the new results to examine future recruiting prospects.

An alternative explanation was that potential supply was as predicted, but that conversion of that supply into enlistments was less effective than before the drawdown.[3] The end of the Cold War and the drawdown might have created more negative attitudes about military service among the general public and the influencers of

---

[2]Throughout this report, we use "supply" and "potential supply" interchangeably to refer to the pool of possible recruits on which the conversion factors operate.

[3]Though there is also a conceptual basis for separating factors influencing supply from those influencing conversion, we distinguish them operationally by whether they impinge on the process before or after initial enlistment intentions are assessed by the surveys. Factors can thus "cross the line." For example, parental advice would be expected to shape the enlistment intentions assessed in the YATS and to continue to influence youth as they near their final enlistment decisions. A similar argument can be made with respect to recruiting resource levels.

youth—such as parents, friends, or school counselors. Such a negative shift, if it occurred, might adversely affect the advice given to youth about joining the military as they near a final enlistment decision as well as recruiter access to youth, for example, in high schools. Another possible supply conversion problem was that the large reduction in recruiting resources during the drawdown could have contributed to important changes in recruiter and resource management practices, such as goaling or the allocation of resources, including the stationing of recruiters. Such changes could affect the ability to cover the whole country and sign potential recruits with the same effectiveness as before the drawdown.

OBJECTIVES AND PLAN OF THE REPORT

This report has two objectives. The first is to update the initial examination of propensity, i.e., potential supply (see Chapter Two). The econometric reanalysis is proceeding, and will be described later in a separate report. The second objective is to present recent research bearing on trends in supply conversion factors (see Chapter Three). Some additional conversion issues, e.g., those related to establishing goals, may be addressed in future reports. Chapter Four summarizes the results and presents our policy recommendations.

Chapter Two

PROPENSITY ANALYSIS OF POTENTIAL SUPPLY

This chapter addresses the supply of potential enlistees, based on our recent analysis of YATS respondents' expressed enlistment intentions ("propensity"). We begin by updating our earlier analyses of actual enlistment rates by stated intention level, which were conducted over a period of several years during the 1980s. The results of the various studies were integrated and summarized in Orvis, Gahart, and Ludwig (1992).

Recall (1) that the extant propensity and econometric models did not predict potential supply problems for FY94, a time when increased difficulties were being reported in some quarters, and (2) that a possible explanation for this inconsistency was that the models were outdated. In this chapter we take another look at the propensity-enlistment relationship, using results through FY95. The analysis updates the earlier work by utilizing more recent propensity and enlistment data; it also uses survival analysis techniques that account for the different lengths of the enlistment follow-up periods associated with the different YATS survey administrations more thoroughly than the approach used in the earlier work did.

Next, we examine propensity trends during the same period. As an integral part of this work, we built an updated model to predict respondents' aptitude from their self-reported demographic and academic characteristics. This allowed us to estimate propensity trends for the primary recruiting market: "high-quality" youth.[1] The new

---

[1] High-quality youth have graduated from high school and score in the upper half of the distribution on the written qualifying test to enter the military. It has been

equation is based on more current survey information and Armed Forces Qualification Test (AFQT) results than our original model, and incorporates a number of new, relevant background questions added to the YATS since the earlier work was carried out. It also remedies deficiencies in the AFQT equation used by DoD in recent analyses of enlistment propensity, which ignored important differences among respondents—such as current year of school—that affected (biased) their estimated AFQT scores. The development of the original equation is discussed in Orvis and Gahart (1989).

The work also included an analysis that accounted for significant changes in the YATS survey and in the youth population numbers used to weight the YATS results. These changes had a significant impact on the propensity estimates reported by DoD in earlier years (see Asch and Orvis, 1994). Our propensity trend analyses control for the effects of these changes: The survey questions and the samples they use are consistent over time, and they incorporate an improved weighting procedure that more accurately reflects results for the national youth population.

The updated procedures to identify results for the high-quality market and the reweighting of the YATS results are discussed in Appendix A. They have been adopted by DoD.

Next we combine the results of the propensity-enlistment and propensity trend analyses to examine the adequacy of potential enlisted supply to meet accession goals in FY94–FY97. We conclude by examining trends in propensity for different racial-ethnic groups.

THE PROPENSITY-ENLISTMENT RELATIONSHIP

The primary measures of propensity to serve in the military (enlistment intention) used by the Department of Defense are assessed in the Youth Attitude Tracking Study (YATS). The YATS is an annual survey of up to 10,000 youth, 16–24 years of age. The 30-minute computer-assisted telephone interview consists of approxi-

---

demonstrated that such youth are more likely to complete their term of service, are more responsive to training, and outperform their lower-quality counterparts. (See, for example, Buddin (1984), Klein, Hawes-Dawson, and Martin (1991), Orvis, Childress, and Polich (1992), and Winkler, Fernandez, and Polich (1992).)

mately 200 questions covering a number of areas of interest to the recruiting community. These include propensity, information on the attitudes of key youth influencers toward military service, patterns of recruiter contacts, and recollections of military advertising, as well as information on employment history, perceptions of military versus civilian job opportunities, and other demographic and academic information. The YATS was initiated in 1975, and given its long history and the prior body of YATS research, we know a great deal about how the answers to its questions relate to actual enlistment decisions.

This report discusses information from a number of the areas assessed in the YATS. Our focus in this chapter is on propensity. There are two primary types of propensity measures assessed in the YATS. The first asks the respondent, "What do you think you might be doing in the next few years?" If he says, "joining the military," he is then considered to have an *unaided mention* of plans for military service. It is "unaided" because the respondent raised the possibility of joining the military himself, without prompting from the interviewer. As we shall see shortly, this is the strongest indicator of the likelihood of joining the military. However, there are a great number of other questions in the YATS that assess propensity. They are of the form, "How likely is it that you will be serving on active duty in the Army (or Navy, Air Force, or Marines) in the next few years?" Respondents are asked to reply "definitely," "probably," "probably not," or "definitely not." Those who say "definitely" or "probably" are considered to have positive propensity for military service, those who say "probably not" or "definitely not" to have negative propensity. The most widely cited measure from the YATS is the "composite active propensity measure," which defines a respondent as having positive propensity if he expresses positive propensity for any of the four active duty services above.

In the 1980s, RAND followed up respondents to the YATS—using Military Entrance Processing Command (MEPCOM) records—and determined their actual enlistment decisions. This provided evidence bearing on the validity of the propensity measures, that is, whether the responses to the measures actually were related to the respondents' eventual enlistment decisions. That work showed a very strong relationship between stated propensity and enlistment. As we noted earlier, however, one possible explanation for the results of last year's initial analysis of recruiting trends was that the evidence linking stated propensity and enlistment was dated; some argued that the relationship might not hold any more. We therefore reestimated that relationship, using updated survey results through the beginning of FY94 (the fall 1993 YATS), a follow-up of MEPCOM enlistment and examination records through the first half of FY95, and statistical techniques that controlled more thoroughly for differences in the observed enlistment window among respondents to the different YATS survey waves (years). (See Appendix A for more detail.)

The reanalysis showed that stated propensity is still very predictive of youth's enlistment decisions. Figure 3 shows this relationship for the group of primary interest to recruiters: high-quality males 16–21 years of age.[2] We find that more than half of such youth with unaided mentions took the written test to qualify for military service (the "production ASVAB"[3]), and about one-third enlisted for active duty. Those rates fall by about half for an intermediate positive group: youth who stated they were likely to serve in one of the four active services but did not have unaided mentions. The rates fall considerably further when we look at those who expressed negative propensity—individuals who told us that they were not likely to serve; in this group only 5% enlisted in the active military. The relationship between stated intention level (propensity) and actual enlistment behavior is especially noteworthy when we consider the young age of the respondents. Many are underclassmen in high school and thus are being asked about a major life decision that is still at least two years away; consequently, since many things could change during that period, we would by no means expect to see a 100% testing rate among the YATS respondents even at the strongest intention level.

In measuring enlisted supply, the strong relationship between positive propensity and enlistment is only part of the picture. The other part involves the very large size of the negative propensity group and

---

[2]The relationship is similar to that demonstrated in the earlier research. In that study, the testing rates among all male youths age 16–21 were 55%, 28%, and 12% for the three categories shown sequentially in Figure 3; enlistment rates were 37%, 15%, and 6% for the same three categories, again among all male youths age 16–21 (Orvis, Gahart, and Ludwig, 1992).

[3]Armed Services Vocational Aptitude Battery, which includes the Armed Forces Qualification Test (AFQT).

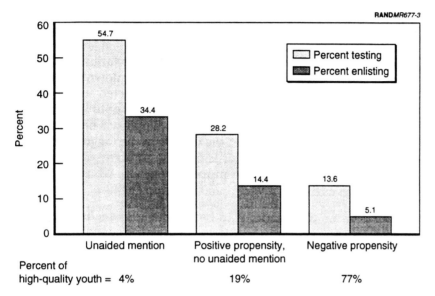

NOTE: The analysis was conducted for 20,200 males age 16–21 who responded
to the fall 1984–fall 1993 YATS surveys.

**Figure 3—Relationship of Stated Propensity to Actual ASVAB Testing and
Enlistment Rates Among High-Quality Youth[4]**

its implications. Among high-quality men 16–21 years old, three-
quarters express negative propensity. Even though very few of these
individuals enlist—about 5%—this group is so big that it accounts for
half of all enlistees. Simply, the negative propensity group is about
three times as large as the two positive propensity groups combined,
whereas its enlistment rate is about one-third as large; thus, the negative propensity group provides approximately half of the enlistees,
with the remaining half provided by the two positive groups together.

_____

[4]In computing these estimates for high-quality youth, we used the AFQT score estimation procedure to weight the YATS respondents and adjusted observed enlistment
rates to account for respondents' inability to enlist if they score below the 31st
percentile on the written qualifying test. The latter step was necessary because the
analysis used results from all of the YATS respondents, whereas, by definition, high-
quality youth would score at or above the 50th percentile on the AFQT. Thus, they
would be eligible to enlist (based on test score). The enlistment rate estimation
procedure is described in Appendix A.

The major role played by the negative propensity group in providing enlistees is significant in properly interpreting trends in aggregate analyses of propensity, for example, in the national level of positive propensity. The strong intention-enlistment relationship dictates that as the positive propensity level trends up or down over time, we will find a corresponding movement in the expected supply of enlistees. So if propensity declines nationally, we should be concerned. However, the magnitude of the decline in supply will be considerably smaller than the magnitude of the decline in the (aggregate) level of positive propensity itself. This is because so many of the enlistees are provided by the negative propensity group, which—by definition—grows as the positive propensity group declines.

Table 1 shows the relationship between a 10% decline in positive propensity and the expected decrease in enlistments, given the enlistment rates shown in Figure 3. We examine two instances of a 10% relative decline in the aggregate level of positive propensity: from 25% to 22.5% and from 10% to 9%. The instances correspond to different types of propensity measures that we might examine. For example, the 25% to 22.5% decline could represent composite propensity for any service, and the 10% to 9% decline, interest in a particular service.[5] In each case, as propensity declines, the right column shows a corresponding decline in expected enlistments. Note, however, that the decline in supply is considerably smaller than the 10% decline in the positive propensity level itself. Note also that the smaller the initial level of positive propensity, the larger the

Table 1

Decrease in Expected Enlistments Compared to Decrease in Positive Propensity Level

10% Decrease in Positive Propensity Level	Expected Decrease in Enlistments
From 25% to 22.5%	–3.9%
From 10% to 9%	–2.0%

[5]The ratio of enlistments among persons stating positive versus negative propensity is comparable for the two types of measures: about 3:1, as stated earlier.

disparity: It takes about twice the percentage drop in propensity on a measure whose positive propensity level is 10% than on one whose average level is 25% to produce the same decline in supply. These relationships should be borne in mind as we now examine national propensity trends since the beginning of the military drawdown.

RECENT TRENDS IN PROPENSITY TO SERVE IN THE MILITARY

Figure 4 shows recent trends in propensity for the primary recruiting group: high-quality males 16–21 years old.[6] As noted, to generate these trend lines we first reestimated the equation used to provide estimates of military interest for the prime market, and we improved the weighting procedures used to make the YATS results nationally representative. (See Appendix A for additional details.) Results are shown for two measures. The first is the most widely known measure from the YATS, the "(four-service) active composite propensity" measure. It shows the percentage of respondents saying that they are likely to serve on active duty in either the Army, Navy, Air Force, or Marine Corps, based on their responses to four questions, one about each service. The other measure illustrates the results for one of the four specific services: respondents saying they are likely to serve in the Army.

Because they ask about different types of propensity—i.e., propensity to serve on active duty in general versus in the Army in particular— the two measures have different rates of positive responses. The issues for the supply analysis, however, involve (1) the slopes of the trend lines during the period being examined and (2) whether the slopes are similar for the two measures. That pattern is quite similar. In each case, as we move from FY89—fall 1988, at the beginning of the last predrawdown year—through FY92, there is a modest increase in the level of positive propensity.[7] This period includes the

---

[6]Throughout this report, propensity estimates or other YATS-based results for "high-quality youth" refer to estimates based on survey data provided by all high school graduates or current high school students, weighted to reflect each such respondent's estimated probability of scoring at or above the 50th percentile on the Armed Forces Qualification Test (see Appendix A).

[7]Tables A.7 and A.8 in Appendix A provide additional propensity information, including annual estimates and their standard errors for FY85–FY95.

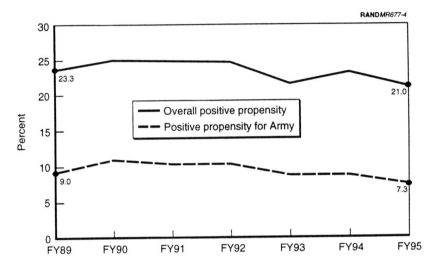

RANDMR677-4

NOTE: Trends based on analysis of results provided by 4,384, 4,792, 3,615, 1,841, 2,005, 1,890, and 2,428 males age 16–21 per wave, respectively. The estimated standard errors are .99, .59, .95, and .55 percent for the FY89 overall and Army measures and the FY95 overall and Army measures, respectively. The timing of the survey coincides with the first quarter of the fiscal year.

Figure 4—Propensity Trends for High-Quality Youth

Gulf War. As the war ends, troops return home, and recruiting resources continue to be cut in connection with the military drawdown, there is a decline in positive propensity from FY92 to FY93,
after which there is some leveling off over the next year. There is
then a second decline between FY94 and FY95, a period coinciding
with declining youth unemployment.

The positive propensity levels assessed in FY95 thus lie below those
of FY89. In the case of the four-service composite measure, the
decline amounts to about 10% in relative terms ($p < .10$). It is nearly
20% for the Army measure ($p < .05$). Does this mean that the Army is
having a bigger supply problem than the military in general? The
answer is "no." The reason involves the magnitude of the expected
decrease in enlisted supply with respect to a decline in the aggregate
positive propensity level (the "elasticity" of enlisted supply with
respect to positive propensity level). As shown in Table 1, the
expected decrease in supply is greater for enlistment intention

measures that have higher aggregate positive propensity levels (e.g., the four-service composite measure as compared to the Army measure). Thus, it takes a bigger *relative* decline in the positive propensity level on the Army-specific measure than would be needed for the four-service composite measure to indicate the same expected decline in supply. In fact, based on the trends and elasticities for the two measures, we would expect the magnitude of the decline in overall supply and in Army supply to be reasonably similar, amounting to less than 5% between FY89 and FY95.[8] As shown in Figure 1, because of the military drawdown, the decline in the required number of non-prior-service accessions during the same period was approximately 35%.

ADEQUACY OF POTENTIAL ENLISTMENT SUPPLY

The magnitude of the decline in positive propensity from (the beginning of) FY89 to FY95 does not suggest a significant supply problem given the corresponding reduction in the annual accession requirement. However, we wanted to analyze more systematically the implications of recent propensity trends for the supply of potential enlistees. We therefore carried out an additional analysis. That analysis had three steps, as shown in Table 2. In the first, we used the proportion of positive and negative responses to various propensity measures and used analyses of the recent enlistment rates associated with those responses to compute the overall expected enlistment rate for the measure and year in question. This is a straightforward matter of taking the proportion of individuals who express positive propensity on that measure in the given year times their expected enlistment rate plus the proportion stating negative propensity times their expected enlistment rate. The sum of the products is the overall expected enlistment rate for the measure and year. (For years following FY95, that year's expected rate is used.)

In the second step, we put the enlistment rate into context by applying it to the size of the male youth population for the year in ques-

---

[8]This holds other factors constant (such as t' size of the youth population). Thus, the measure actually indexes the change in the   ment rate. Below we deal explicitly with changes in the youth population and in th accession requirement. These factors must be incorporated to assess the adequacy of enlisted supply.

Table 2

Steps in Computing Index of Enlisted Supply/Requirement Ratio

1. Compute expected enlistment rate from propensity level

2. Account for size of youth population and for accession requirement

$$\frac{\text{Youth population} \times \text{expected enlistment rate}}{\text{High-quality accession requirement}}$$

3. Compare expected supply/requirement ratio with analogous predrawdown ratio (FY89)

tion—which provides an estimate of enlisted supply. We then divided the estimated supply by the requirement for non-prior-service high-quality male accessions in the given year. Actual accession numbers were used to define the requirement through FY94. From FY95 forward, we used the latest applicable accession goals based on the Program Objective Memorandum submissions from the four services. This calculation provides a ratio of the potential enlisted supply relative to the requirement for the given year. The applicable propensity, population, and accession numbers are presented in Appendix A.

We are not so much interested in the value of that ratio for one year as in how the ratio is changing over time. Specifically, we desire an index that tells us how the ratio for FY95 compares with its predrawdown value. We chose FY89 as the yardstick because it was the last predrawdown year, a time before the resource cuts when recruiting was good. In step three, we computed that index by dividing the ratio for the year of interest (e.g., FY95) by the analogous ratio for the baseline year (FY89). In making this calculation we hope to see an index value larger than one. That would suggest that supply increased relative to the requirement for high-quality accessions, whereas an index value of less than one would suggest that supply decreased relative to the requirement.[9]

---

[9]This analysis was carried out for the primary (and most difficult) recruiting market: high-quality male youth. Older YATS respondents (ages 22–24) contribute a much smaller percentage of enlistments than their proportion of the population—and thus

Table 3 shows the index values generated by dividing the ratio of
supply to requirement for the indicated year by the analogous ratio
for FY89. We begin with FY94, to assess the similarity of these results
to those reported in our preliminary analysis (see Asch and Orvis,
1994). As noted, the new results draw on an updated model of actual
enlistment rates by stated enlistment intention level, on a new equation to identify trends for the high-quality market, on a revised
weighting scheme for the YATS to make it nationally representative,
and on methodological refinements in estimating the ratio of supply
to requirement. Still, given that the updated intention level–
enlistment results are similar to those found in the original work, as
noted earlier, we also would expect the findings of the supply/
requirement ratio analysis to be similar to those reported in FY94.

The results in Table 3 bear out this expectation; they validate and
extend the earlier results. As we reported earlier (Asch and Orvis,
1994), the FY94 index for the DoD as a whole is approximately 1.25,
meaning that supply exceeded its predrawdown level by about 25%
relative to the requirement ($p < .05$). Similarly, as we look across the
services, all the indexes stand at about 1.0 or higher, suggesting an
adequate supply of potential enlistees.[10] Indeed, the index values for
the Army and Air Force are significantly greater than 1.0 ($p < .05$),

----

were excluded from the propensity trend analyses. However, they are eligible to be
recruited in meeting the non-prior-service high-quality male accession requirement
(denominator), and we therefore included them in the enlistment rate and population
estimates (numerator). We used census figures for the male youth population 16–24
years of age. We did not have reliable population figures for the subset of male high-
quality youth. This difference should have little effect, if any, on the index value of
current (or near-term) supply to FY89 supply. Not only is the change in population
small over this period, but the population trend should be highly similar for the high-
quality and male youth groups.

To estimate the enlistment rates used in the numerator, we conducted a series of
survival analyses analogous to those mentioned earlier. (See Appendix A for details.)
Depending on the particular supply estimate being assessed, the rates reflect enlistment for active duty in the military or enlistment in a particular service. Unlike the
earlier results shown in Figure 3, which are based on estimates of lifetime enlistment
rates, the present analysis estimated enlistments over a one-year period. Separate
rates were estimated according to age, education status (e.g., whether in school), and
propensity level. The results for these groups were then weighted according to their
respective proportions of the youth population and combined to provide an overall
one-year enlistment rate for the given service and year.

[10]Supply met requirements in FY89. Here, we view supply as "adequate" if it is
sufficient to meet the given year's accession requirement given the FY89 potential
supply-to-enlistment conversion rate.

Table 3

Potential High-Quality Enlisted Supply: Index of Supply/Requirement Ratio Relative to Predrawdown (FY89) Ratio (Fall 1988–1994 YATS, Males, Age 16–24)

Year	DoD	Army	Navy	Marine Corps	Air Force
FY94	1.25	1.50	1.02	1.01	1.17
FY95	1.09	1.28	1.09	0.79	1.10
FY96	1.01	1.04	1.01	0.84	1.11
FY97	0.93	0.88	1.02	0.77	1.13

NOTE: Figures are for indicated year versus FY89 and control for the difference in accession requirements for the two years.

indicating an increase in potential high-quality enlisted supply relative to the requirement. The ratio is highest for the Army, because it had the largest drawdown in accessions by FY94 relative to FY89.

As we move from FY94 to FY95, there is some decline in the supply index on average. This primarily reflects the decline in enlistment propensity between the beginning of FY94 and FY95; the postdrawdown accession requirement was similar for the two years. Still, the index remains above 1.0, suggesting adequate potential supply. There is one exception to this pattern: The Marine Corps recruiting plan for FY95 called for an increase in accessions of some 15% relative to FY94, exceeding the FY89 accession requirement. This accounts for the larger decline in the Marine Corps index and its value of less than 1.0 (p < .05).[11]

The analyses for FY96 and FY97—a time of increased accession requirements—show a different pattern. Whereas for FY94 and FY95 the supply of potential enlistees appears to have exceeded accession requirements for the DoD, this is no longer the case. By FY96, we see the index values falling toward 1.0, with the Marine Corps index remaining significantly below 1.0 (p < .05). The exception is the Air Force, whose planned accession increase will not occur until FY99,

---

[11]The small declines in positive propensity for the Marine Corps and in the youth population between FY94 and FY95 do not account for the larger decline in the Marine Corps index. The population change applies to all of the services, and the propensity decline for the Marine Corps was, if anything, smaller than for the other services.

according to the POM; we would thus not expect a drop in the supply index until then.

In FY97, the situation worsens for the Army and Marine Corps due to the increase in their accession requirements. As a result, the DoD, Army, and Marine Corps supply index values now all lie below 1.0, the Navy's barely above it. This suggests that by FY97, potential enlisted supply for the DoD may be below that of the predrawdown period (relative to the requirement), significantly so for the Army and Marine Corps ($p < .05$).

While we should not take the index values as exact, the overall pattern prompts concern. The difficulties reported by recruiters in FY94 and FY95 came at a time when the analysis suggests that potential supply generally was well above its predrawdown level, relative to the requirement. This suggests that the services continue to have conversion problems in enlisting the potential supply in the market. As we move from FY94 to FY97, the substantial reduction in the values of the ratios further suggests that we may be adding a supply problem to the conversion problem. The supply problem will be exacerbated to the extent that propensity worsens, since the estimates were (necessarily) based on the propensity levels available at the time of the analysis (through FY95).[12] Thus, the overall pattern suggests the possibility of noteworthy difficulties in the recruiting market.[13]

RECENT TRENDS IN PROPENSITY TO SERVE AMONG MINORITY GROUP MEMBERS

Last, we examine additional trends in youth interest in joining the military according to race-ethnicity. We find that although there has been a decline in propensity overall, that decline has been much steeper for African-Americans than for other race-ethnic groups. Appendix A shows results for propensity to serve on active duty (in the Army, Navy, Air Force, or Marine Corps). Between FY89 and FY95, positive propensity fell by about 10% in relative terms among

---

[12]Subsequent information indicates that overall propensity for high-quality male youth remained unchanged from FY95 to FY96.

[13]A sensitivity analysis indicates that the foregoing results are similar whether we use FY89 or FY88 as the predrawdown baseline year.

whites. Over the same period, the propensity decline was much steeper for blacks, falling from just under 34% to about 23%, a decline of about one-third in relative terms. Results for Hispanic youth on the overall measure are similar to those of whites.

Figure 5 presents the Army results. The bottom trend line, for whites, shows about a 10% decrease in positive propensity for the Army, similar to the decline in overall propensity noted above. However, the decline for African-Americans is significantly steeper (p < .05), with positive propensity falling from 19.4% in FY89 to only 8.4% in FY95 (p < .05). That is a relative decline of nearly 60%. The decline among Hispanic youth is intermediate, at just under 30%.

The trends are of concern both with respect to meeting post-drawdown high-quality accession requirements in general and with respect to the ability to continue to maintain recent (higher) social representation levels for African-Americans in particular. At this

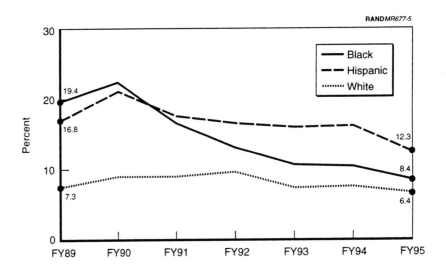

NOTE: Trends based on analysis of results provided by 4,384, 4,792, 3,615, 1,841, 2,005, 1,890, and 2,428 males age 16–21 per wave, respectively, of whom approximately 75–80% were white, 9% African-American, and 9% Hispanic.

Figure 5—Trends in Positive Propensity to Serve in Army Among High-Quality Youth in Different Race-Ethnic Groups

point, we do not know the reason for the greater decline. It could relate to possible changes over this period in college plans or economic opportunities for the different groups. However, the preliminary results have not supported that hypothesis. Those analyses did show a greater perception among African-American youth of danger in military service, as compared with whites, and a corresponding greater reluctance to serve under conditions involving potential exposure to combat. (See Appendix A.) Some in the recruiting community have theorized that the perceptions of greater danger can be traced to concerns about safety and potentially unequal exposure to combat conditions raised by leaders in the African-American community during Operation Desert Shield/Storm (ODS). However, data from the YATS and from the "Monitoring the Future" survey suggest that in some instances differences in perceptions of risk and in willingness to volunteer for combat predate ODS and have not abated since then. These results and important limitations on the time periods and relevant YATS questions for which trends can be generated make a clear interpretation of the differences impossible at this time; still, the possible combat-related nature of the differences raises questions about the efficacy of some recent military advertising that stresses combat themes. We are pursuing additional data to help address the reasons for the large downturn in propensity.

Chapter Three

CONVERSION OF POTENTIAL SUPPLY

In Chapter Two we presented evidence bearing on trends in the supply of potential enlistees. In this chapter we examine the portion of our recent recruiting research that deals with the conversion of that supply. Specifically, we will look at three areas: First, we will examine what those analyses suggest about trends in the rates of enlistment-related discussions between youth and their key influencers—their parents and friends—and in the counsel they have received about the desirability of joining the military. Those results are drawn from analyses of the Youth Attitude Tracking Study. Second, we will examine reports from the DoD Recruiter Survey (see Appendix B) about rates of contact with the families of potential recruits and about the level of support recruiters believe they are getting from high school counselors. That survey was administered in fall 1989, 1991, and 1994 (beginning of FY90, FY92, and FY95). In each of those years, there were responses from 1,000 to 2,000 production recruiters with a year or more of experience who were recruiting for the active services. Last, we will present evidence concerning recruiter access to youth in high school and patterns of contacts with recruiters. Access to youth could be reduced by downturns in societal attitudes toward the value of the military; if so, that might be presaged by evidence of more negative counsel concerning enlistment from key influencers, including school counselors. Alternatively, if there is a contact problem, it could be one that was created from drawdown-related reductions in the number of recruiters and in the number and locations of recruiting stations. Since the country has remained the same size, some of these actions may have caused recruiters to become more isolated from local markets.

DISCUSSIONS BETWEEN YOUTH AND KEY INFLUENCERS

Recent results from the YATS do show a decline in reported discussions with key influencers about the possibility of serving in the military. Figure 6 shows the percentage of youth reporting discussions with their father, mother, and friends within the last twelve months about that possibility. The results for the three measures are similar and statistically significant ($p < .05$). The steepest decline occurred in the percentage of youth saying they had spoken to their friends about the possibility of serving: from about 27% in FY91 (fall 1990) to about 18% in FY95 (fall 1994), a decline of one-third in relative terms.

Does this indicate an additional negative impact on potential supply beyond that reflected in the propensity trends shown in Chapter Two? The answer is "apparently not." If we consider the actual enlistment rate for those who report discussions with a particular influ-

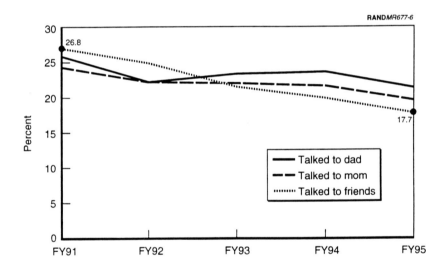

NOTE: Trends based on analysis of results provided by 3,615, 1,841, 2,005, 1,890, and 2,428 males age 16–21 per wave, respectively. The starting and ending percentages for friends, mothers, and fathers are (26.8%, 17.7%), (24.2%, 19.4%), and (25.7%, 21.3%) respectively. The standard errors are (.84%, .88%), (.75%, 1.09%), and (.81%, 1.01%) respectively.

Figure 6—Trends in Percentage of High-Quality Youth Reporting Discussions with Influencers About Joining the Military

encer in the past twelve months—assessed in both the current and prior YATS research—along with the analogous enlistment rate for those who say they have not had such discussions, then the expected effect on enlisted supply of the changes in the proportions in Figure 6 amounts to about the same reduction predicted from the propensity analysis.[1]

Although the decline in conversations with influencers is consistent with the decline in propensity, we might worry whether youth who do talk to influencers get more negative advice about joining the military than they used to. This could reduce enlistment rates. Figure 7 clearly suggests that this concern is unfounded. According to the YATS data, among youth discussing possible military service with their parents or friends, the proportions reporting that these persons advised them not to join the military have remained very flat (and statistically equivalent) since fall 1991.

RECRUITER REPORTS OF DISCUSSIONS WITH AND SUPPORT FROM KEY INFLUENCERS

We can examine some analogous results from the DoD Recruiter Surveys. In fall 1994, one of the questions asked recruiters about the recent level of contact they had with the families of potential enlistees as compared with the period before the drawdown-related resource cuts (about 1992). As shown in Figure 8, most of the recruiters reported that they had about the same level of contact as before the

---

[1]Due to changes in the YATS questions, meaningful analysis of recent trends in the rates of discussions with influencers must be limited to the FY91–FY95 surveys, and in counsel received, to FY92–FY95. We have focused on the implications of propensity trends over the same period when comparing the implications of the propensity and influencer results for enlisted supply. The results are very similar. For example, if we use FY91 as the base year and compute the enlisted supply index for FY97 (see discussion of Table 3), the index value is 0.92 based on whether the respondent stated a positive versus a negative propensity to serve in the military, and it is 0.94 based on whether or not he talked to a friend about serving. Also, as is true of the propensity results, discussions with influencers about serving in the military declined more among minority youth; in this case, however, the difference between African-American and white youth is not statistically significant.

It also is possible that youth are talking less about life plans in general with influencers, and that this could contribute to the decline in the rate of discussions about joining the military. The YATS does not provide data on such analogous discussions, however.

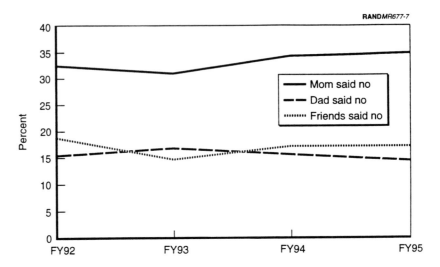

RANDMR677-7

NOTE: Trends based on analysis of results provided by approximately 900 males age 16–21 in FY92 who discussed the possibility of military service with the indicated influencer; samples for FY93–FY95 are approximately half that size. The starting and ending percentages for friends, mothers, and fathers are (18.4%, 16.8%), (32.3%, 34.5%), and (15.1%, 14.0%) respectively.

Figure 7—Trends in Percentage of High-Quality Youth Receiving Negative Counsel from Influencers About Joining the Military

cuts: nearly 70% said so. The proportion reporting less contact was somewhat greater than that reporting more contact, so the overall pattern showed some decline ($p < .05$).[2] This decline could be attributable to the general decline in propensity, the effects of resource cuts (including the number of recruiters), or both.

Recruiters were not asked about the advice given to youth by their parents or friends, but they were asked about another potentially important influencer: high school counselors. What were the high school counselors telling youth about the desirability of enlisting?

_____

[2]The significance test can be conducted as a t-test of the mean being less than zero— say, for assigned response values of –1, 0, and 1—or as a sign test of the difference in the number of "less contact" versus "more contact" responses. Both tests yield Z score approximations exceeding 6.2 (in absolute value).

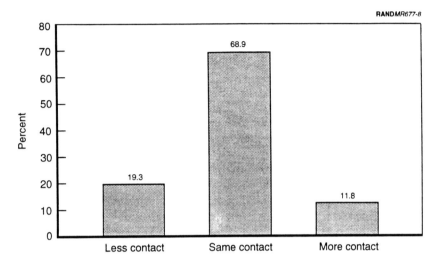

RANDMR677-8

SOURCE: Recruiter Survey fall 1994, production recruiters with 1+ years.
NOTE: The analysis was conducted for 2,152 recruiters.

Figure 8—Recruiter Reports of Contact with Families of Potential Enlistees

Figure 9 presents these results. The results are similar to those re-ported by the YATS respondents for their families. Comparing the results of the Recruiter Survey in fall 1994 with those in fall 1991 (when these questions were asked for the first time), we find no downturn in the proportion of recruiters saying that counselors would encourage seniors to talk to them about the possibility of en-listing. Similarly, we find no downturn in their reports concerning whether counselors would advise students to consider the military as a means of getting money for education.

Overall, then, both the YATS and Recruiter Survey results show some decline in rates of discussion with influencers about military service. However, the declines do not appear to pose problems for enlisted supply beyond those identified by the decline in positive propensity levels assessed in the YATS; that is, they do not point to (additional) problems in the conversion of potential supply. Rather, the declines are consistent with the overall decline in stated propensity; more-over, neither dataset suggests increased problems with the counsel being given by influencers about serving in the military.

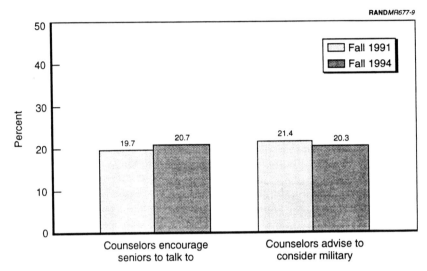

RANDMR677-9

SOURCE: Recruiter Surveys, production recruiters with 1+ years.

NOTE: The analysis was conducted for 1,177 recruiters in fall 1991 and 2,152 recruiters in fall 1994.

Figure 9—Trends in High School Counselors' Advice to Students About Joining the Military

RECRUITER ACCESS TO STUDENTS AND CONTACTS WITH YOUTH

We now examine recruiter access to youth at high schools. We noted earlier that reduced access to youth could result from changes in societal values in which military service is viewed less favorably. However, the results just described on parents', friends', and school counselors' advice given to youth show no such trend; instead, the percentages of parents, friends, and counselors encouraging youth to consider military service have remained about the same over the past few years. Consequently, we might expect that access has remained constant as well. The data support this expectation.

In the fall 1994 Recruiter Survey, respondents were asked whether they were making the same number of visits to their local high schools, more visits, or fewer visits than before the drawdown-related cutbacks. As shown in Figure 10, most recruiters reported that they were making about the same number of visits: nearly 60% said that. Of the remaining 40%, more recruiters indicated that they were making more visits rather than fewer visits (24% versus 16%). The overall pattern thus shows some increase in visits (p < .05). This does not suggest increased restrictions in access to students. That indication is supported by a variety of additional measures, to which we now turn.

Figure 11 shows trends in access to high school students according to a number of criteria. The first four measures reflect results reported by recruiters in the DoD Recruiter Survey. The last measure reports results from a different database: a record of high school ASVAB administrations and access to institutional ASVAB results maintained by the Military Entrance Processing Command (see Appendix B). In each case, we compare the 1994 results to those reported for the same measure in 1991.[3]

In comparing results for the fall 1994 and fall 1991 Recruiter Surveys, we see virtually no movement on any of the four measures, reminiscent of the earlier results for advice given by influencers. Over the three-year period, the same percentages report that they are free to talk to seniors about enlisting, that they can display their materials in school, that they are invited into classes to talk about the military as a career, and that they are invited to career days at high schools. Moreover, those results are cross-validated by results from the high school ASVAB database. One of the variables in that database gives detailed indications of the types and extent of restrictions, if any, on access to students and their test results that are placed on recruiters. Figure 11 shows the percentage of the records with no restrictions on access to the students or their test results. That amounts to some 85% of the students in 1991, and there is no change in access in 1994.

---

[3]The fall 1989 DoD Recruiter Survey did not include these measures. The MEPCOM database does include records for 1989; however, the access results for 1989 and 1991 are very similar, and thus we have chosen to present the 1994 versus 1991 comparison to preserve consistency with the period covered by the Recruiter Survey comparisons. More generally, because the downturn in propensity and reported recruiting difficulties occurred after fall 1991, the trends in access between 1991 and 1994 cover the period of interest.

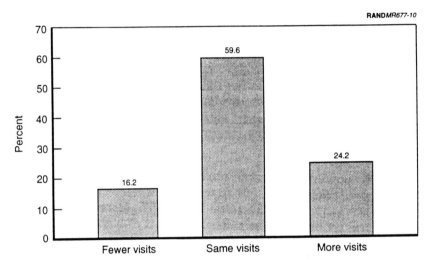

RAND*MR677-10*

SOURCE: Recruiter Survey fall 1994, production recruiters with 1+ years.
NOTE: The analysis was conducted for 2,152 recruiters.

Figure 10—Recruiter Reports of Visits to High Schools

We observed earlier that contacts with high school students could decline because recruiter access was being restricted by the schools or, alternatively, because of actions taken by the services to cope with resource cuts, such as reducing the numbers of recruiters and stations. Although the foregoing analyses do not indicate an increase in access restrictions, we still wanted to examine directly possible changes in patterns of recruiter-youth contacts.

Figure 12 presents results from that analysis. The trend lines show the estimated percentage of high-quality male youth reporting contacts with recruiters within the last twelve months. The trend covers fall 1990 (FY91) to fall 1994 (FY95).[4] According to the YATS data, that rate has remained relatively constant among high school graduates; the small increase is not statistically significant. However, as shown by the upper trend line, among (high-aptitude) high school students there has been a significant decline in contact over this period. The

_____

[4]Changes in the YATS questions preclude meaningful comparisons with the fall 1989 survey.

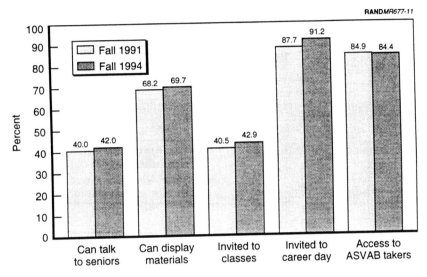

RANDMR677-11

SOURCE: Recruiter Surveys, MEPCOM High School ASVAB Database.

NOTE: The Recruiter Survey analyses were conducted for 1,177 recruiters in fall 1991 and 2,152 recruiters in fall 1994. ASVAB results are based on 15,067 schools in 1991 and 13,321 schools in 1994.

Figure 11—Trends in Recruiter Access to High School Students

rate of contact fell from about 47% to 37% (a decline of 20% in relative terms, t = 4.7, p < .05).[5] When considered together with the maintenance of contact with graduates, this decline suggests a shift in recruiter focus toward the graduate market.

Although the overall decline in recruiter contacts is consistent with the decline in positive propensity, the story appears to be more complex and, as noted, to involve increased emphasis on the high school graduate market. It is possible that reductions in the number of recruiters and stations have increased the number of schools an individual recruiter is responsible for, thereby causing some of the markets to become more remote and thus reducing the feasible

---

[5]As we would expect given the greater decline in propensity among African-American youth, their recruiter contacts declined to a greater extent than did those among white youth (p < .10). This pattern applied both to graduates and high school students.

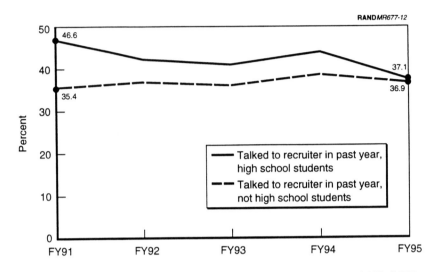

RAND*MR677-12*

NOTE: Trends based on analysis of results provided by 3,615, 1,841, 2,005, 1,890, and 2,428 males age 16–21 per wave, respectively. Sample sizes among high school students are 1,828, 965, 1,071, 959, and 1,229. Sample sizes among those not in high school are 1,787, 876, 934, 931, and 1,199. The starting and ending percentages for the overall sample are (41.0%, 37.0%) ($p < .05$ for the difference).

Figure 12—Trends in Recruiter Contacts with High-Quality Youth

number of recruiter visits to at least some high schools. That is, an individual recruiter could be visiting as many or more schools as in the past, but the total number of visits could have declined. A second, related possibility is that recent difficulties in meeting monthly recruiting targets have caused episodic shifts in focus to the "direct" graduate market. This would be especially likely during the middle of the academic year, when recruiters need to ship recruits to Basic Training but students cannot yet go.

Additional evidence suggesting a decline in recruiter contacts with high school students is provided by recent trends in high school ASVAB testing. Figure 13 indicates that between school year 1987–1988 and school year 1993–1994 there was a decline in the total number of students testing, from about 1.1 million per year to about 850,000 per year. The bottom trend line shows that the number of schools participating in the program has declined from about 15,700

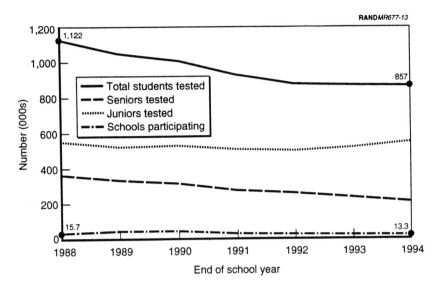

RAND*MR677-13*

SOURCE: MEPCOM High School ASVAB Database.

NOTE: The starting and ending numbers for the four trend lines (in thousands) are (1,122.3, 856.9), (547.7, 538.4), (354.0, 202.4), and (15.7, 13.3) from top to bottom, respectively. The average student population per high school testing was 553 in 1988 and 570 in 1994; thus, there is no reduction in student body size that might explain the decline in the number of students tested per school.

Figure 13—Trends in Rate of High School ASVAB Testing

to 13,300 during the same period. That is a relative decline of some 15%; it reflects a significant reduction but is smaller than the decline in number of students tested, which amounts to 24%. Thus, both the number of high schools participating in the ASVAB testing program and the rate of student participation at those schools appear to have declined.[6]

As noted above with respect to contacts with high school students, these declines could have resulted from reductions in the number of recruiters and stations, which may have reduced the feasible number

_____

[6]Very little of the decline in the number of students testing or schools participating can be explained by changes in the size of the youth population or in the number of high schools during this period, which were minimal.

of visits to high schools. At the same time, high school ASVAB tests are cited consistently by recruiters as one of the most important sources of leads. Thus, it also is possible that the reduction in tests has contributed to the decline in recruiter contacts with high school students, rather than merely being coincident with it. If this is so, some reassurance is provided by the second trend line in Figure 13, which shows that testing has not declined among juniors. Juniors represent the primary test group, both in terms of size and the opportunity for recruiters to identify top prospects, discuss the option of military service, and influence the youth's post–high school plans. Testing has declined among seniors (third trend line) and underclassmen (not shown).

Chapter Four

SUMMARY AND RECOMMENDATIONS

SUPPLY OF POTENTIAL ENLISTEES

In analyzing potential supply, we reestimated the model that relates the stated intentions of survey respondents to their actual enlistment decisions. The reanalysis corroborates the findings of the preliminary research. Intentions stated in the YATS still predict enlistments; moreover, the rates of enlistment for different intention groups are consistent with those derived in the earlier analysis. Analysis of recent trends in propensity for high-quality male youth reaffirms that predicted supply for FY94 and FY95 generally exceeded its FY89 level relative to accession requirements. In other words, if anything, the supply of potential high-quality enlistees increased since the beginning of the drawdown—when recruiting was good—relative to the accession requirement.[1] Thus, the recent difficulties reported by recruiters in FY94 and FY95 came at a time when potential supply appears to have been adequate; this suggests continuing problems in converting supply into enlistments.

Notwithstanding the results for FY94–95, there has been some downturn in high-quality youth's interest in military service. When that downturn is coupled with the large postdrawdown increase in accession requirements for the Army and Marine Corps, we find that potential supply could fall short of its predrawdown levels. Thus, by FY97 we may have to overcome a supply problem in addition to con-

---

[1] The Marine Corps is an exception to this pattern. Its goal of increasing non-prior-service accessions by 15% in FY95 caused its supply ratio to fall well below 1.0. It later reduced this accession goal.

version issues. The downward trend is greater for minority groups, particularly African-Americans, whose propensity has fallen far more steeply than that of other race and ethnic groups.

CONVERSION OF POTENTIAL SUPPLY

Although the data show reductions in the rate at which potential high-quality recruits discuss military service with key influencers such as family members and friends, the magnitudes of the reductions are consistent with the general reduction in propensity. That is, the size of the predicted decrease in high-quality enlisted supply is similar for the two indicators. Thus, these reductions do not appear to constitute an additional problem. Still, we might worry if the advice received by youth who do have such discussions had become more negative. While the results are not conclusive, we find no evidence that the counsel provided by parents or friends has become more negative over the past several years. Similarly, the Recruiter Survey results suggest that the advice given to students by school counselors on military service has remained constant during this period.

A related issue involves access to high school students. As we indicated earlier, had there been a downturn in societal or influencer favorability toward the military, we might have expected more difficulty in gaining access to students in high school. As just noted, however, we found no evidence of such a downturn in attitudes. Similarly, we find little change in recruiters' ability to gain access to high schools. According to the DoD Recruiter Survey, recruiters, if anything, report increased visits to local high schools. Moreover, there is virtually no change in recruiters' reported ability to gain access to high schools to talk to seniors about enlisting, display their materials, give talks in classes, or be present at career days. Similarly, results from the MEPCOM database on high school ASVAB administrations suggest no decline in recruiters' access to students and test results over the past several years.

Although gaining access to high schools does not appear to have become more difficult, other data suggest that there nonetheless has been a decline in the rate of contacts between recruiters and high school students. Relative to high-quality high school graduates—for whom the rate of contact has remained relatively constant—a significant downturn is reflected by reports from current high school students about contacts with recruiters during the last twelve months. The reduced level of contact is consistent with lower propensity, but the fact that it is more concentrated among high school students suggests the importance of other factors.

One reason for the reduced contact could involve reductions made during the drawdown in the numbers of recruiters and stations, which could have made some markets more remote and reduced the feasibility of maintaining predrawdown visit levels. A second factor could involve episodic shifts in the recruiting focus to high school graduates rather than students, in order to meet short-term shipping goals during times of increased recruiting difficulty. An additional possibility involves the downturn in the rate of high school ASVAB administrations, which are known to be a good source of leads. This downturn could result from reduced recruiter presence at high schools, or it could be contributing to the reduced level of contacts with high school students.

RECOMMENDATIONS

We find the total pattern of results to be consistent with declining propensity plus continuing difficulties in converting potential supply into enlistments. The conversion problems may result from a variety of factors; as noted, one of these is possible isolation from some markets. Based on these interim results, our recommendation is to consider increases in advertising, educational benefits, and the number of recruiters; this should help ensure that the DoD will meet current recruiting goals and be positioned to meet the increased accession requirements in FY97.[2] It is important to act soon, considering the proximity of the increase and the lead time required to put the resources in place. The recommended resources have been shown to be the most cost-effective resources for recruiting high-

---

[2]Meeting the increased accession requirement also could be facilitated by reducing the percentage of high-quality recruits or by increasing the number of female or prior-service accessions. There is a downside to each of these alternatives; for example, lower-quality recruits have higher training costs and are more likely to attrite. In this report, we assume the services intend to maintain their programmed accession goals for high-quality, male, and non-prior-service recruits.

quality youth.[3] Moreover, they are flexible: They can be increased or decreased as needed.

To further enhance cost-effectiveness and because demand-side practices—such as resource allocation decisions, enlistment options, and goaling—also are important determinants of recruiting success, we recommend that DoD identify specific shortages that need to be remedied before increasing resources, to the extent feasible. This includes several factors: For example, are shortages concentrated in specific types of jobs, or are they endemic in many specialties? Different responses suggest different approaches to targeting the resources, with different potential costs. Similarly, are the shortages concentrated in specialties with limited benefits—for example, are Army shortages concentrated in MOSs that do not offer the maximum educational benefit value—or are they present in specialties that already offer maximum benefits (e.g., the Army College Fund)? In the latter case, the implication would be to increase the maximum value of the benefit; in the former, it would suggest increasing the number of specialties offering the maximum current benefit. Similar arguments can be made with respect to other options, for example, different terms of service. The basic question is how the presence or absence of shortages in occupational specialties covaries with the options that are available. These patterns should be analyzed to obtain guidance on the types of actions and magnitudes of incentives that may improve the recruiting picture, and that will do so in a cost-effective manner.

By analogy, a similar strategy should be considered with respect to possible increases in recruiters and stations. Specifically, over the past few years the military has reduced the number of recruiters and stations. Thus, it is likely that recruiters have become more distant geographically from certain markets, and may be able to make fewer contacts. Similarly, the smaller recruiting force may not be able to maintain the same presence in high schools that existed before the drawdown-related resource reductions. The question becomes whether recruiting shortages are more pronounced in markets that have become more isolated or have experienced larger reductions in the recruiting force, or whether they are prevalent throughout the

---

[3]These results are summarized in Asch and Orvis (1994).

country. The answer to this question would provide guidance on the desired number of recruiters and stations as well as their locations.

YOUTH ATTITUDE TRACKING STUDY

The primary source of data for the research documented in this report is the Youth Attitude Tracking Study (YATS). This is the principal measure used by the Department of Defense to assess youth interest in military service. The survey is a 30-minute computer-assisted telephone interview that includes about 200 questions. The YATS is conducted in the fall, and has been administered to approximately 5,000 to 10,000 youth of age 16 to 24 per year. It was initiated in 1975.

In this appendix we present additional results from that survey. We also describe a number of important refinements that we made to the procedures for weighting the survey data to derive nationally representative results and for estimating results for the prime (high-quality) recruiting market. The refinements made to the YATS in the course of this study were necessitated by a number of significant modifications that occurred in the YATS and related datasets during the late 1980s and early 1990s. We needed to account for these changes to produce comparable nationally representative estimates for the past ten years.

WEIGHTING PROCEDURE FOR YATS SURVEY DATA

A new weighting procedure for the YATS was required as a consequence of a number of important changes that occurred in the Census Bureau's Current Population Survey, which is used to generate population control totals, and in the YATS survey itself. In this section we indicate the changes that took place and describe the new procedures we developed to account for them. The procedures described below were developed in collaboration with the Office of the Secretary of Defense—in particular, the Office of Accession Policy and the Defense Manpower Data Center—and Westat (the YATS contractor). They have been adopted as the official weighting procedures, and the YATS results for the past ten years have been reweighted accordingly.

Changes in the Youth Attitude Tracking Study

During the period fall 1991–1993, the YATS sample comprised two groups of roughly equal size: one that had participated in the YATS in the previous year(s)—a "panel" group—and a second that was new to the survey that year. The reason for reinterviewing a part of the previous year's sample was that, in principle, it could reduce costs and provide additional information on changes in youth attitudes over time. However, the follow-up rates of about 60% to 65% for the panel component of the YATS were low. This is problematic because it very likely resulted in a nonrandom sample of individuals. In particular, the enlistment propensities for individuals in the panel were significantly lower than for youth being interviewed for the first time. The absolute difference in propensity between the two groups was about six percentage points, which corresponds to a relative difference of about 20% to 25%. DoD was unable to explain the variance in propensity between the members of the panel component and the rest of the sample using a variety of demographic, educational, and other variables. To produce comparable samples for the past ten YATS administrations—most of which did not include panels—and to deal with the apparent nonresponse bias in the panel data, the most reasonable course of action was to omit from the sample the individuals who were reinterviewed. This required a subsequent readjustment of the sample weights to generate nationally representative estimates.

Other changes to the YATS sample involving the eligibility of college students occurred in fall 1990. Before that year, all youth who resided at a college dormitory were ineligible for inclusion in the survey. Beginning with fall 1990, youth living in dormitories while attending college were contacted for the survey if the interviewers obtained their telephone numbers from their parents (i.e., from a noninstitutional telephone number). Although in theory these youth may respond differently than nondormitory residents, they were not removed from the sample because it was not possible to identify them. An additional change in the YATS in fall 1990 involved the inclusion of youth who had completed more than two years of college; previously, such persons were excluded because they do not represent the prime recruiting market for enlisted personnel. To maintain comparability over time, we removed these youth from YATS survey data collected in fall 1990 or afterward.

Changes in Population Estimates

Sample results need to be adjusted, that is, the results for different groups need to be weighted, to reflect differences between the composition of the sample and that of the population it is supposed to represent. In general terms, the weights are ratios of the proportion of the represented population falling within a given group to its proportion in the sample.

In recent survey waves, the weights for the YATS were calculated using population estimates from the Census Bureau's Current Population Survey (CPS)—disaggregated by age, race-ethnicity, and education level—that were published in the series *Educational Attainment in the United States*. The use of the data from this publication for weighting the YATS is of concern for two reasons. First, the population estimates were based on published data from the March CPS survey. Because the YATS is conducted in the fall, there is a six- to seven-month discrepancy between the survey and the population estimates. This is troublesome for adjusting a survey sample to reflect the school status of the youth population. Most seniors still in high school in March become graduates by the fall; in contrast, some underclassmen in high school in the spring do not return to school the following fall. Moreover, the percentage of youth in college also differs for the two time periods. Second, because the population estimates were based on a single month of data, they exhibited an excessive degree of variability across survey years.

Our response to these concerns was to generate population estimates based on weighted averages of data from the three CPS surveys conducted during the fall months corresponding most closely to the time that the YATS is usually fielded (i.e., September–October–November). This new procedure also allowed us to take into account annual changes in the racial-ethnic, education, and age composition of the population. Previously, education composition was assumed to remain constant over longer periods, and only racial-ethnic and age totals were changed annually.

In addition, a major change occurred in the CPS in 1992 regarding the treatment of youth who had attended some college or were currently attending college. Prior to 1992 these youth were categorized as either having completed up to two years of college or more than two years of college. Beginning in 1992, these two CPS questions were combined into a single measure indicating whether an individual had some college education, but no degree. Before the change in the CPS, the information on education from this survey corresponded well with the YATS, which historically collected information on youth who had up to two years of college education. The change in the CPS education question necessitated an alteration of the weighting scheme. Our solution was to use the CPS number to weight all youth in the YATS with any college education and then to use the information in the YATS to remove individuals with more than two years of college.

The final issue in developing the new weighting scheme was to select an appropriate weighting algorithm. There were two contenders: a fully crossed scheme, in which a target population is provided for each cell (corresponding to one gender-race/ethnicity-education-age group), and a raked scheme, in which only row and column totals are matched (corresponding to an individual gender-age or race/ethnicity-education cell). These two procedures provided similar estimates of enlistment propensity—the key YATS measure—but the variances with the fully crossed scheme were substantially larger. This difference was especially notable when calculating propensities for subgroups. We consequently used the raked scheme for weighting the YATS.

ESTIMATION OF TRENDS FOR THE PRIME RECRUITING MARKET

The YATS is the primary survey used by the Department of Defense to assess youth interest in serving in the military and to help design recruiting and advertising strategies. DoD's emphasis is on recruiting high-quality youth: persons graduating (with diplomas) from high school and capable of scoring at or above the 50th percentile (Categories I–IIIA) on the Armed Forces Qualification Test (AFQT). Given that emphasis, most youth surveys have an important short-coming: they do not identify such persons. Thus it is not possible to examine trends for the group of primary recruiting interest.

Below we describe and apply a method of using the information contained in national youth surveys—and the YATS in particular—to estimate the probability that respondents would score in Categories I–IIIA if they took the AFQT. The method can be used for a variety of purposes. It is possible to generate estimates for the prime market or to compare estimates for higher- versus lower-quality youth on factors such as enlistment propensity, future plans, recruiter contacts, awareness of military advertising and enlistment incentives, and demographic characteristics.

The new equation represents an updated version of the procedure developed previously by RAND. (The development of the original procedure is discussed in Orvis and Gahart (1989).) The new equation uses more current survey and AFQT information, and it takes advantage of new questions that have been added to the YATS survey. (See Table A.1 for the questions used.) Specifically, as is true for the analysis of enlistment rates, we used a dataset matching the survey results from fall 1984 through the beginning of FY94 (the fall 1993 YATS) with MEPCOM enlistment and examination records through the first half of FY95. The MEPCOM data provided the actual AFQT scores of YATS respondents who took the AFQT to qualify for military service. This amounts to about 20% of the male respondents aged 16–21. We used a small number of replicate records to correct for the fact that youth interested in taking the AFQT are screened by recruiters, resulting in progressive underrepresentation of the population below the 20th percentile.

We distinguished the test takers scoring in AFQT Categories I–IIIA from those scoring below the 50th percentile. We then used logistic regression to model this outcome (see Tables A.1 and A.2). In the earlier analysis, we worried about selection bias due to the limited observation of test scores, and we used a two-equation maximum likelihood procedure to correct for the specification problems that might result. However, that work showed only a very small correlation between the error terms of the testing and AFQT equations. The implication was that the use of a single equation to estimate the probability of attaining a high AFQT score would have been adequate. In the current instance, preliminary analyses confirmed the earlier finding, showing little effect on the coefficients of the predictor variables when an instrument for the likelihood of testing (propensity) was included. Still, to be conservative, we retained the measure in the new equation. That equation is shown below. It corrects limitations of a revised equation used by DoD in recent years.

Table A.1

YATS Questions Used to Model AFQT Score and Corresponding Variable Names

Variable Name in YATS	Variable Name in Table A.2
Q406 Q404A Q408	Dropped out (dropped out of high school)
Q404A	Some college (completed some college)
Q408	In college (in college now)
Q700	GPA (grade category)
Q713A	Dad's ed (< 12, 12, 13–15, 16+ years)
Q713B	Mom's ed (< 12, 12, 13–15, 16+ years)
	Completed
Q702	algebra elem (elementary algebra)
Q703	geometry
Q704	bus math (business math)
Q705	computer sci (computer science)
Q706	algebra int (intermediate algebra)
Q707	trig (trigonometry)
	Plans to take
Q704	bus math (business math)
Q706	algebra int (intermediate algebra)
Q404A	freshman, sophomore, junior, senior (current year of (high) school)
Q510 Q511 Q512 Q513	pos comp prop (positive composite active propensity)
STFIPS	north cent, south, west (census region of residence)
Q714 Q715	Hispanic, black, other (race-ethnic group)
Q701	college prep (in/attended college prep. school)
Q402	female
Q402 Q706	fem x plans alg int (female x plans to take intermediate algebra)
Q402 Q714 Q715	fem x black

NOTE: With the exception of GPA, Dad's ed, and Mom's ed, all variables are dichotomous with values equal to 1 for above answer and 0 otherwise. The YATS variable names are taken from the fall 1994 survey.

Table A.2

Results of Logistic Regression to Predict Likelihood of Scoring in AFQT Categories I–IIIA

Variable	Parameter Estimate	Standard Error	Pr > Chi-Square	Mean
Intercept	−3.4472	0.1680	0.0001	
Dropped out	0.0908	0.0866	0.2944	0.1666
Some college	0.4565	0.1112	0.0001	0.1007
In college	0.5321	0.0989	0.0001	0.1390
GPA	0.2076	0.0251	0.0001	4.3092
Dad's ed	0.1821	0.0356	0.0001	2.2706
Mom's ed	0.2061	0.0378	0.0001	2.2099
Completed				
algebra elem	0.9836	0.0825	0.0001	0.7781
geometry	0.6410	0.0662	0.0001	0.5467
bus math	−0.2419	0.0599	0.0001	0.4077
computer sci	0.3235	0.0662	0.0001	0.2839
algebra int	0.2639	0.0697	0.0002	0.4818
trig	0.4896	0.0837	0.0001	0.2115
Plans to take				
bus math	−0.3131	0.1468	0.0330	0.0456
algebra int	0.1959	0.1361	0.1501	0.0635
Freshman	0.6900	0.4738	0.1453	0.0036
Sophomore	0.3014	0.1722	0.0801	0.0351
Junior	0.8088	0.1018	0.0001	0.1416
Senior	0.7026	0.0880	0.0001	0.1862
Pos comp prop	−0.3340	0.0611	0.0001	0.4910
North central	0.2656	0.0885	0.0027	0.2371
South	0.1293	0.0809	0.1098	0.4237
West	0.1500	0.0983	0.1270	0.1581
Hispanic	−1.0024	0.0991	0.0001	0.0893
Black	−2.0205	0.0926	0.0001	0.1908
Other	−1.0620	0.1660	0.0001	0.0295
College prep	0.6190	0.0635	0.0001	0.6699
Female	−0.1540	0.0972	0.1129	0.1269
Fem x plans bus math	1.2589	0.4632	0.0066	0.0049
Fem x black	0.5349	0.2151	0.0129	0.0285

NOTE: The regression is based on 7,515 cases. The mean predicted probability of scoring in AFQT Categories I–IIIA is 0.524. The chi-square for the model is 2,930 (df = 29, p < .0001).

The logistic regression equation thus is estimated as

$$\text{probtest} = \alpha + \beta_1 x_1 + \beta_2 x_2 + \ldots + \beta_n x_n.$$

The probability of scoring in AFQT Categories I–IIIA (upper half) is

$$e(\text{probtest}) / (1 + e(\text{probtest})).$$

To assess the usefulness of the estimation, we compared the *predicted probability* that AFQT takers will score at the 50th percentile or higher with the *actual proportion* of test takers scoring in Categories I–IIIA. In this type of analysis, the estimation procedure should be capable of generating a full range of predicted probabilities, that is, the predictions should be distributed fully between 0 and 1, rather than clustered narrowly around the mean probability. Table A.3 shows the distribution of respondents in the matched YATS-MEPCOM database across the predicted probability categories. Ten comparisons of predicted and actual results are shown, corresponding to the decile of the predicted probability of scoring in Categories I–IIIA. The distribution supports the usefulness of the procedure. The predicted probabilities are well distributed across the entire possible range.[1]

SURVIVAL ANALYSIS OF INTENTION-ENLISTMENT RELATIONSHIP

YATS-MEPCOM matches made by RAND in the 1980s provided the first evidence bearing on the validity of the propensity measures, that is, whether the responses to the measures actually were related to the respondents' eventual enlistment decisions. That work showed a strong relationship between stated propensity to serve in the military (intention) and enlistment, at both the individual and aggregated (e.g., regional) levels (see Orvis, Gahart, and Ludwig, 1992).

---

[1]An additional measure of usefulness would be to apply the regression coefficients to a separate set of individuals analogous to those used to estimate the equation and then to compare the predicted and actual probabilities of scoring in AFQT Categories I–IIIA. Because we had done so earlier and found close agreement between the predicted and actual results for a similar equation, we did not repeat that analysis here. See Orvis and Gahart (1989) for a discussion of the earlier analysis.

Table A.3

Distribution of YATS Respondents Across Predicted AFQT Scores

Predicted Probability of Scoring in Categories I–IIIA	Number of Respondents	% Scoring in Categories I–IIIA
$.9 < p \le 1.0$	596	96.1
$.8 < p \le 0.9$	869	88.0
$.7 < p \le 0.8$	630	76.0
$.6 < p \le 0.7$	582	64.4
$.5 < p \le 0.6$	473	55.8
$.4 < p \le 0.5$	464	48.5
$.3 < p \le 0.4$	429	43.6
$.2 < p \le 0.3$	531	29.4
$.1 < p \le 0.2$	536	18.5
$0 < p \le 0.1$	368	9.5

As stated in Chapter One, our initial analysis (Asch and Orvis, 1994) relied in part on that intention-enlistment relationship to infer that the recruiting difficulties reported in FY94 should not be attributed to a shortage of potential enlisted supply; if anything, the potential supply of enlistees appeared to have increased relative to the recruiting mission, as compared with the period just prior to the military drawdown. We have noted that one possible explanation for those results was that the evidence linking stated propensity to enlistment was dated; some argued that the relationship might not hold any more. We therefore reestimated that relationship, using updated survey results through the beginning of FY94 (the fall 1993 YATS), a follow-up of MEPCOM enlistment and examination records through the first half of FY95, and additional statistical techniques.

The reanalysis showed that stated propensity still is very predictive of youth's enlistment decisions. The relationship, highlighted in Table A.4, is both strong and similar to the results of the earlier research.

The table shows the annual and total enlistment rates (in percent) for each of the three propensity groups discussed in the main text; the numbers correspond to those shown in Figure 3. The enlistment rates are estimates for high-quality youth. This was accomplished by excluding high school dropouts from the analysis and by adjusting the raw enlistment rates to account for the severe restrictions placed

Table A.4

Annual and Total Enlistment Percentages by Propensity Level

Propensity Level	Number of Cases	Number Tested	Enlisted by 12 Months	Enlisted at 12–24 Months	Enlisted at 24–36 Months	Enlisted at 36–48 Months	Enlisted after 48 Months	Total Enlisted
Positive propensity, unaided mention	1,301	712	11.0	11.5	6.7	2.5	2.7	34.4
Positive propensity, no unaided mention	5,034	1,422	2.9	4.7	2.9	1.7	2.2	14.4
Negative propensity	13,865	1,890	1.0	1.4	1.0	0.6	1.1	5.1

on enlisting persons who score below the 31st percentile on the AFQT—Categories IV and V. The active duty military recruits very few youth from Category IV and is prohibited by law from recruiting those scoring in Category V. No such restrictions are placed on recruiting high-quality youth. Since the survival analysis procedure that we used could not be directly weighted by an individual's predicted probability of scoring at or above the 31st percentile, the adjustment was carried out as follows:

- First, we divided the YATS respondents in each of the three propensity groups into quintiles according to their estimated probabilities of scoring in AFQT Categories I–IIIA. This allowed a rough aptitude categorization of the entire group (not just those who took the AFQT). For those in each quintile who took the AFQT, the actual percentages scoring in Categories I–IIIA and I–IIIB were then calculated.

- The raw enlistment rate for each quintile was then divided by the proportion of test takers in the quintile who scored in Categories I–IIIB—those potentially eligible to enlist. The result was, within each quintile, an estimate of the percentage of youth who would have enlisted if they were eligible to do.

- A high-quality enlistment rate for the propensity group was then estimated by averaging the adjusted enlistment rates for the quintiles, weighting each according to the number of Category I–IIIA test takers in the quintile.[2]

We noted that youth interested in taking the AFQT also are screened. Based on an analysis of the observed distribution of scores—specifically, the underrepresentation of scores below the 20th percentile— we estimate that the unscreened test-taking rates would be 64.9%, 34.3%, and 15.5% for the three propensity groups; the raw rates are 54.7%, 28.2%, and 13.6%.

An analogous procedure was carried out for the DoD and for each active service in the computation of the potential enlisted supply/

---

[2]Let q_i = number of respondents in quintile i; b_i = proportion of AFQT-takers in quintile i scoring in Categories I–IIIB; a_i = proportion of AFQT-takers in quintile i scoring in Categories I–IIIA; and e_i = enlistment rate for respondents in quintile i. The operation summarized above may be expressed as $(\sum_i q_i a_i e_i / b_i)/(\sum_i q_i a_i)$.

accession requirement indices discussed in Chapter Two (see Table 3). In that instance, we used the overall or service-specific propensity measure, and we estimated the 12-month enlistment rate (in the DoD or applicable service) for high-quality males aged 16–24. We performed separate "survival" analyses for each propensity level and, within level, for each of the following eight high school (year) or high school graduate (age) groups: sophomore, junior, or senior in high school; age 18, 19, 20, 21, or 22–24 high school graduate.

Recall that the interviews are conducted in the fall; for each school year–age group, we thus apply the 12-month enlistment rates for the applicable propensity measure and level to estimate enlistments during the fiscal year beginning at the time of the YATS survey. For example, we use the fall 1994 YATS results and 12-month enlistment rates to estimate enlisted supply for FY95. The population numbers used in the supply/requirement index estimates are drawn from the Bureau of the Census Current Population Survey (by gender and age). In computing the index, actual accessions are used for FY88, FY89, and FY94. For FY96 and FY97, the non-prior-service accession requirements from the FY96–01 POM submissions are apportioned to males and females according to the services' specifications in the FY95–97 OSD Budget (BES) submissions; the BES itself is used for the (near-term) FY95 accession requirement. The high-quality proportions for the services and the DoD in FY94 are applied to FY95–97. Table A.5 shows the population and accession numbers used in computing the indices in Table 3. Table A.6 shows the standard errors of the enlisted supply index results, which were estimated using bootstrapping procedures.

RACE-ETHNIC GROUP DIFFERENCES IN PROPENSITY AND PERCEPTIONS OF MILITARY JOBS

The high-quality male positive propensity percentages aggregated over the eight school year–age groups are shown in Table A.7, which also distinguishes them by race-ethnicity. Negative propensity levels equal 100 minus the corresponding positive level. We have labeled the propensities according to the YATS wave in which they were assessed. Table A.8 shows the corresponding standard errors, which were estimated using bootstrapping procedures.

Table A.5

Population and Accession Numbers Used in Index of Potential High-Quality Enlisted Supply
(In thousands)

Year	Accession Requirement					Youth Population
	DoD	Army	Navy	Marine Corps	Air Force	
FY88	139.0	52.1	40.1	20.6	26.2	17,976
FY89	135.3	51.1	36.4	20.1	27.7	17,724
FY94	99.1	32.1	28.4	20.3	18.4	16,833
FY95	102.9	33.2	26.7	23.3	20.0	16,741
FY96	111.0	40.7	28.7	21.8	19.7	16,641
FY97	119.0	48.0	28.1	23.7	19.2	16,544

Table A.6

Standard Errors of Index of Potential High-Quality Enlisted Supply

Year	DoD	Army	Navy	Marine Corps	Air Force
FY94	.070	.078	.067	.068	.079
FY95	.055	.073	.073	.054	.069
FY96	.051	.059	.067	.057	.070
FY97	.047	.050	.068	.052	.072

NOTE: Figures are for indicated year versus FY89 and control for the difference in accession requirements for the two years.

Last, we include additional data from the Youth Attitude Tracking Study dealing with perceptions of risk in the military and desire to serve in combat. We noted in Chapter Two the greater decline in propensity for African-American youth relative to white youth. This trend is clearly visible in Table A.7. It is of concern both with respect to meeting postdrawdown high-quality accession requirements and recent social representation levels for African-Americans. At this point, we do not know the reason for the greater decline. As noted, although in principle it could relate to possible changes over this period in college plans or economic opportunities for the different groups, the preliminary results have not supported that hypothesis.

Table A.7

Fall 1984 (FY85)–Fall 1994 (FY95) Positive Propensity Levels for High-Quality Males Age 16–21 by Race-Ethnicity and Service
(In percent)

Propensity Assessed	1984	1985	1986	1987	1988	1989	1990	1991	1992	1993	1994
High-quality male youth, age 16–21											
Any service	20.9	19.4	22.9	24.0	23.3	24.9	24.6	24.5	21.3	23.0	21.0
Army	8.3	8.0	9.0	9.5	9.0	10.7	10.1	10.1	8.5	8.5	7.3
Air Force	12.0	10.8	12.4	14.4	13.1	13.7	12.6	12.4	10.9	11.0	9.6
Marines	5.9	5.8	6.8	7.8	7.3	8.2	6.9	8.2	7.7	8.3	7.9
Navy	7.4	6.8	8.2	9.8	9.0	9.8	8.7	8.5	8.0	7.1	6.5
Cases	4,159	4,204	4,529	4,678	4,384	4,792	3,614	1,841	2,005	1,890	2,428
White respondents											
Any service	19.2	17.0	20.3	20.6	21.3	22.0	22.6	22.1	19.3	21.4	19.4
Army	7.2	6.5	7.4	7.4	7.3	8.6	8.6	9.3	7.2	7.3	6.4
Air Force	10.8	9.4	10.4	12.1	11.9	12.1	11.4	10.6	9.7	9.6	8.7
Marines	5.4	4.7	6.0	6.3	5.8	6.5	6.3	7.1	6.5	7.3	7.2
Navy	6.7	5.9	7.7	8.1	8.1	8.5	8.2	7.7	6.8	6.5	6.0
Cases	3,295	3,207	3,437	3,605	3,372	3,698	2,805	1,463	1,532	1,401	1,813
African-American respondents											
Any service	32.8	36.3	40.1	39.7	33.8	41.5	28.1	36.7	22.6	26.1	23.0
Army	17.0	19.7	23.2	23.0	19.4	22.1	16.4	12.9	10.3	10.2	8.4
Air Force	21.1	21.1	23.2	24.8	17.2	24.5	12.7	23.4	11.1	13.0	10.7
Marines	7.3	13.3	12.4	12.1	15.1	16.1	6.9	11.3	10.1	10.3	7.1
Navy	10.2	11.5	14.5	15.9	11.2	15.7	9.4	8.7	9.0	8.5	8.8
Cases	484	498	564	493	464	469	304	161	154	175	232
Hispanic respondents											
Any service	36.9	30.0	36.0	38.4	35.4	40.0	36.5	36.9	34.8	33.0	31.2
Army	17.3	13.6	15.4	15.8	16.8	20.9	17.4	16.3	15.8	16.0	12.3
Air Force	21.7	15.4	22.6	19.4	21.1	19.9	20.3	20.5	18.8	19.0	14.6
Marines	12.9	13.9	11.5	14.9	16.0	19.1	11.0	16.7	15.6	14.5	13.5
Navy	14.0	12.7	9.7	15.1	14.4	15.9	12.1	13.7	15.4	10.3	8.3
Cases	283	388	372	415	411	468	315	138	193	203	237

Table A.8

Standard Errors for Fall 1984 (FY85)–Fall 1994 (FY95) Positive Propensity Levels for High-Quality Males Age 16–21

(In percent)

Propensity Assessed	1984	1985	1986	1987	1988	1989	1990	1991	1992	1993	1994
High-quality male youth, age 16–21											
Any service	0.75	0.72	0.72	0.78	0.99	0.80	0.81	1.13	1.03	1.02	0.95
Army	0.48	0.48	0.48	0.58	0.59	0.50	0.56	0.76	0.67	0.68	0.55
Air Force	0.62	0.56	0.56	0.68	0.67	0.57	0.59	0.86	0.78	0.89	0.70
Marines	0.40	0.36	0.41	0.43	0.62	0.43	0.44	0.72	0.68	0.70	0.60
Navy	0.48	0.44	0.51	0.60	0.74	0.54	0.47	0.72	0.69	0.69	0.54
Cases	4,159	4,204	4,529	4,678	4,384	4,792	3,614	1,841	2,005	1,890	2,428
White respondents											
Any service	0.77	0.76	0.85	0.75	1.13	0.88	0.90	1.16	1.10	1.14	1.03
Army	0.51	0.47	0.51	0.48	0.58	0.50	0.53	0.81	0.67	0.77	0.60
Air Force	0.63	0.59	0.60	0.62	0.75	0.62	0.68	0.81	0.81	0.93	0.79
Marines	0.42	0.35	0.45	0.39	0.59	0.46	0.47	0.75	0.72	0.81	0.60
Navy	0.52	0.48	0.57	0.52	0.83	0.55	0.52	0.72	0.75	0.75	0.60
Cases	3,295	3,207	3,437	3,605	3,372	3,698	2,805	1,463	1,532	1,401	1,813
African-American respondents											
Any service	2.88	3.30	2.88	3.49	3.50	3.42	2.93	5.12	3.78	3.78	3.36
Army	2.34	2.60	2.39	2.90	3.46	2.44	2.45	2.70	2.54	2.31	1.90
Air Force	2.73	2.63	2.30	3.15	2.36	2.98	2.26	4.78	3.15	3.01	2.47
Marines	1.27	2.15	1.69	1.80	3.49	2.46	1.50	3.06	2.94	2.43	2.03
Navy	1.80	1.62	2.06	2.49	2.12	2.32	2.15	2.41	2.81	2.21	2.35
Cases	484	498	564	493	464	469	304	161	154	175	232
Hispanic respondents											
Any service	4.05	2.85	3.21	3.25	3.69	2.66	3.07	5.21	3.82	3.83	3.47
Army	2.82	2.09	2.32	1.86	2.47	2.19	2.54	4.27	2.86	3.06	2.33
Air Force	3.42	1.99	2.81	2.17	3.02	2.21	2.55	4.60	2.98	3.36	2.48
Marines	2.50	2.20	1.93	2.10	2.54	2.22	1.97	4.32	3.11	2.33	2.49
Navy	2.32	1.85	1.69	3.24	2.25	2.19	1.94	3.11	2.78	2.06	1.88
Cases	283	388	372	415	411	468	315	138	193	203	237

Those analyses did show a perception among all youth of considerable danger and personal risk in military service, a greater perception of danger among African-American youth as compared with whites, and a corresponding greater reluctance to serve under conditions involving potential exposure to combat. Results from these analyses are shown below in Tables A.9 to A.11.[3]

Some have attributed the greater African-American propensity decline to ODS-related concerns. Where comparisons are possible, however, data from the YATS and from the "Monitoring the Future" survey—which, taken together, span the ODS period—suggest that differences in perceptions of risk and in willingness to volunteer for combat predate ODS and have not abated since then. These results and important limitations on the time periods and relevant YATS questions for which trends can be generated make a clear interpretation of the differences impossible at this time. Still, together with the greater decline in propensity among African-American youth, the (YATS) results in Tables A.9 to A.11 raise questions about the efficacy of military advertising that stresses combat themes.

Table A.9

Response to "Life in the Military Involves Great Danger and Personal Risk."
(In percent)

Response	White Respondents	African-American Respondents
Strongly agree	22.5	45.2
Somewhat agree	42.7	32.8
Neither	12.7	6.8
Somewhat disagree	17.6	7.7
Strongly disagree	4.5	7.5
Number of cases	9,014	1,027

NOTE: High-quality males, 16–21 years old, fall 1990–1994 YATS combined.

---

[3]Sample size varies from table to table principally because the different questions were asked in different numbers of years and because they were put to different portions of the survey sample.

Table A.10

Intention to Volunteer for Service in the Event of War
(In percent)

Response	White Respondents	African-American Respondents
Definitely volunteer	10.4	4.4
Probably volunteer	39.1	35.4
Probably not volunteer	36.9	28.6
Definitely not volunteer	13.6	31.6
Number of cases	7,846	883

NOTE: High-quality males, 16–21 years old, fall 1990–1994 YATS combined. The question reads, "If you felt it were necessary for the U.S. to fight in some future war, what would be the likelihood you would volunteer to serve in the military? Would you say that you would . . ."

Table A.11

Desire to Serve in Combat-Related Job to Secure Better Promotion Opportunity
(In percent)

Response	White Respondents	African-American Respondents
Definitely volunteer	10.9	5.5
Probably volunteer	38.1	29.5
Probably not volunteer	34.1	27.9
Definitely not volunteer	16.8	37.1
Number of cases	1,813	232

NOTE: High-quality males, 16–21 years old, fall 1990–1994 YATS combined. The question reads, "If you were in the military today and knew that chances for promotion were better in assignments that might take you into combat, do you think you would . . . for those kinds of assignments?"

OTHER DATASETS USED IN THE ANALYSIS

In this appendix we describe the datasets that we used in the analysis in addition to the Youth Attitude Tracking Study. These include the Department of Defense Recruiter Survey, the Military Entrance Processing Command High School ASVAB database, and the "Monitoring the Future" survey.

RECRUITER SURVEY

The Department of Defense Recruiter Survey was fielded in fall 1989, 1991, and 1994. The survey was commissioned originally to address concerns about recruiting improprieties and poor recruiter quality of life. Quality-of-life dimensions include recruiting goals; management issues at various levels; work hours and annual leave; location and safety of residence and work; job preparation and training; living conditions and family life; and overall satisfaction with recruiting and the military. The scope of the survey has increased greatly over time: it examined the effects of the Gulf War in fall 1991, downsizing in 1991 and 1994, access to youth in 1994, and the role of high school ASVAB testing in 1994.

The fall 1989 survey collected information from active duty recruiters in the Army, Navy, Air Force, and Marine Corps. In fall 1991, Guard and Reserve components were added, and the Coast Guard was added in fall 1994. For the analysis presented in this report, we limited our attention to active duty production recruiters in the Army, Navy, Air Force, and Marine Corps with one or more years of experience. These selection criteria resulted in samples of 1,554 in 1989,

1,177 in 1991, and 2,152 in 1994; the corresponding response rates are 80%, 74%, and 71%.

HIGH SCHOOL ASVAB DATABASE

The High School ASVAB database is assembled and maintained by MEPCOM. It contains information on high school administrations of the Armed Services Vocational Aptitude Battery (from which the AFQT score is computed) for every high school in the United States during the period covering school year 1987–1988 to school year 1993–1994. Information from approximately 21,500 high schools is included in the database; these include public, private, and parochial schools. The total number of high schools in the United States has remained relatively constant between 1988 and 1994.

The high school ASVAB testing program is administered by the regional Military Entrance Processing Station (MEPS). A MEPS educational specialist contacts local high schools to arrange the testing date and site. High school counselors organize student attendance, while the MEPS arranges all other details, including the proctoring of the tests by local recruiters. The test is provided at no charge to the schools.

Each school is allowed to determine recruiter access to student testing data. Restrictions on access range from a time delay before recruiters can contact youth (anywhere from 60 days to the remainder of the school year), to prohibition of telephone solicitations, to a complete restriction on contact. It turns out, however, that approximately 85% of test takers have no restrictions on recruiter access to their test data, and that this rate has been fairly constant over the period covered by the database.

Variables in the database include the number of participating schools, the number of test takers, and the number of students by grade. Also included are reasons why schools did not participate in testing; whether they were ineligible for testing and, if so, why; whether testing of students at each grade was mandatory; and the restrictions, if any, placed on recruiter access by the schools.

MONITORING THE FUTURE

"Monitoring the Future" (MTF) is a nationally representative survey of high school seniors that is conducted on an ongoing basis by the University of Michigan's Institute for Social Research. The aim of this annual survey is to collect information on changes in attitudes, values, behaviors, and lifestyle among youth in the United States. Approximately 1,300 variables are included in the survey. The study, which began in 1975, surveys students in the spring of each year. Sample sizes are large: there are over 16,000 students in each wave, distributed among roughly 125 schools. The design of the study to focus on high school seniors means that all students who drop out before the spring of their senior year are omitted from the survey.

Attitudes toward (and the use of) drugs, tobacco, and alcohol are the areas that are covered in greatest depth in the survey. Other topics that are investigated include attitudes about government, social institutions, race relations, changing roles for women, educational aspirations, occupational aims, marital and family plans, and a variety of social, family, and demographic background factors. For this study, the variables of principal interest were measures of youth attitudes toward the military. These included views about the armed services and the use of military force, as well as personal plans for military service.

Whites and African-Americans are the only two racial-ethnic groups that are identified in the survey. Individuals who identify themselves as belonging to all other racial and ethnic groups are combined in a single residual category.

BIBLIOGRAPHY

Asch, Beth J., *Navy Recruiter Productivity and the Freeman Plan*, Santa Monica, CA: RAND, R-3713-FMP, June 1990.

Asch, Beth J., and Bruce R. Orvis, *Recent Recruiting Trends and Their Implications: Preliminary Analysis and Recommendations*, Santa Monica, CA: RAND, MR-549-A/OSD, 1994.

Asch, Beth J., and Lynn A. Karoly, *The Role of the Job Counselor in the Military Enlistment Process*, Santa Monica, CA: RAND, MR-315-P&R, 1993.

Ajzen, Icek, and Martin Fishbein, *Understanding Attitudes and Predicting Social Behavior*, Englewood Cliffs, NJ: Prentice-Hall, 1980.

Bachman, Jerald G., Lloyd D. Johnston, and Patrick M. O'Malley, *Monitoring the Future: A Continuing Study of the Lifestyles and Values of Youth, 1992*, Ann Arbor, MI: Survey Research Center, University of Michigan, 1993.

Bentler, Peter M., and G. Speckart, "Attitudes Cause Behaviors: A Structural Equation Analysis," *Journal of Personality and Social Psychology*, Vol. 40, 1981, pp. 226–238.

Bentler, Peter M., and G. Speckart, "Models of Attitude-Behavior Relations," *Psychological Review*, Vol. 86, 1979, pp. 452–464.

Berner, J. Kevin, and Thomas V. Daula, *Recruiting Goals, Regime Shifts, and the Supply of Labor to the Army*, U.S. Military Academy, working draft, February 1993.

Berryman, S. E., R. M. Bell, and W. Lisowski, *The Military Enlistment Process: What Happens and Can It Be Improved?* Santa Monica, CA: RAND, R-2986-MRAL, May 1983.

Bray, R. M., et al., *Youth Attitude Tracking Study II, Fall 1983*, Research Triangle Park, NC: Research Triangle Institute, 1986.

Brown, C., "Military Enlistments: What Can We Learn from Geographic Variations?" *American Economic Review*, Vol. 75, 1985, pp. 228–234.

Brunner, G. L., *The Importance of Volunteer Status: An Analysis and Reliability Test of Survey Data*, Santa Monica, CA: RAND, R-0717-PR, October 1971.

Buddin, R. J., *Analysis of Early Military Attrition Behavior*, Santa Monica, CA: RAND, R-3069-MIL, July 1984.

Chow, Winston K., and J. Michael Polich, *Models of the First-Term Reenlistment Decision*, Santa Monica, CA: RAND, R-2468-MRAL, September 1980.

Congressional Budget Office, *Quality Soldiers: Costs of Manning the Active Army*, Washington, D.C.: U.S. Congress, 1986.

Cotterman, Robert F., *Forecasting Enlistment Supply: A Time Series of Cross Sections Model*, Santa Monica, CA: RAND, R-3252-FMP, July 1986.

Daula, T. V., and D. A. Smith, "Recruiting Goals, Enlistment Supply, and Enlistments in the U.S. Army," in *Army Manpower Economics*, C. L. Gilroy (ed.), Boulder, CO: Westview Press, pp. 101–123, 1986.

Daula, Thomas V., and D. Alton Smith, "Estimating Enlistment Models for the U.S. Army," in *Research in Labor Economics*, Vol. 7, Greenwich, CT: JAI Press, 1985, pp. 261–310.

Davidson, Andrew R., and James J. Jaccard, "Population Psychology: A New Look at an Old Problem," *Journal of Personality and Social Psychology*, Vol. 31, 1975, pp. 1073–1082.

Dertouzos, J., *Recruiter Incentives and Enlistment Supply*, Santa Monica, CA: RAND, R-3065-MIL, May 1985.

Dertouzos, J. N., J. M. Polich, A. Bamezai, and T. Chestnutt, *Recruiting Effects of Army Advertising*, Santa Monica, CA: RAND, R-3577-FMP, January 1989.

Fernandez, R. L., *Enlistment Effects and Policy Implications of the Educational Assistance Test Program*, Santa Monica, CA: Santa Monica, CA: RAND, R-2935-MRAL, September 1982.

Fishbein, Martin, and Icek Ajzen, *Belief, Attitude, Intention and Behavior: An Introduction to Theory and Research*, Reading, MA: Addison-Wesley, 1975.

Fiske, Susan T., and Shelley E. Taylor, *Social Cognition*, Reading, MA: Addison-Wesley, 1984.

Fredericks, A. J., and D. L. Dossett, "Attitude-Behavior Relations: A Comparison of the Fishbein-Ajzen and the Bentler-Speckart Models," *Journal of Personality and Social Psychology*, Vol. 45, 1983, pp. 501–512.

Haggstrom, G. W., *Logistic Regression and Discriminant Analysis by Ordinary Least Squares*, Santa Monica, CA: RAND, P-6811, March 1982.

Heckman, J. J., "The Common Structure of Statistical Models of Truncation, Sample Selection, and Limited Dependent Variables, and a Simple Estimator for Such Models," *Annals of Economic and Social Measurement*, Vol. 5, 1976, pp. 475–492.

Hiller, John R., *Analysis of Second-Term Reenlistment Behavior*, Santa Monica, CA: RAND, R-2884-MRAL, September 1982.

Hom, P. W., and C. L. Hulin, "A Competitive Test of the Prediction of Reenlistment by Several Models," *Journal of Applied Psychology*, Vol. 66, 1981, pp. 23–29.

Hom, P. W., R. Katerberg, and C. L. Hulin, "Comparative Examination of Three Approaches to the Prediction of Turnover," *Journal of Applied Psychology*, Vol. 64, 1979, pp. 280–290.

Hosek, J. R., and C. E. Peterson, *Enlistment Decisions of Young Men*, Santa Monica, CA: RAND, R-3238-MIL, July 1985.

Jaccard, James, and Andrew R. Davidson, "A Comparison of Two Models of Social Behavior: Results of a Survey Sample," *Sociometry*, Vol. 38, No. 4, 1975, pp. 497–517.

Juster, Thomas F., *Anticipations and Purchases: An Analysis of Consumer Behavior*, Princeton University Press, Princeton, NJ, 1964.

Keenan, K. M., "Reasons for Joining and Early Termination of Service in WRAC," in M. Tuck (ed.), *How Do We Choose? A Study in Consumer Behavior*, London: Methuen, 1976.

Klein, Stephen P., J. A. Hawes-Dawson, and Thomas Martin, *Why Recruits Separate Early*, Santa Monica, CA: RAND, R-3980-FMP, 1991.

Kmenta, J., *Elements of Econometrics*, New York: Macmillan, 1971.

Maddala, G. S., *Limited-Dependent and Qualitative Variables in Econometrics*, Cambridge, UK: Cambridge University Press, 1983.

Mare, Robert D., Christopher Winship, and Warren N. Kubitschek, "The Transition from Youth to Adult: Understanding the Age Pattern of Employment," *American Journal of Sociology*, Vol. 90, 1984, pp. 326–358.

Market Facts, Inc., *Youth Attitude Tracking Study*, Spring 1976–Fall 1982 Reports, August 1976–May 1983.

Office of the Assistant Secretary of Defense for Manpower, Reserve Affairs, and Logistics, *Profile of American Youth: 1980 Nationwide Administration of the Armed Services Vocational Aptitude Battery*, Washington, D.C., 1982.

Olsen, R. J., "A Least Squares Correction for Selectivity Bias," *Econometrica*, Vol. 48, 1980, pp. 1815–1820.

Orkand Corporation, *Parents' Perceptions of Their Influence on Youths' Enlistment Decisions*, Office of the Assistant Secretary of Defense (Manpower, Reserve Affairs, and Logistics), March 1983.

Orvis, Bruce R., *Forecasting Enlistment Actions from Intention Information: Validity and Improvement*, Santa Monica, CA: RAND, N-1954-MRAL, December 1982.

Orvis, Bruce R., *Analysis of Youth Cohort Enlistment Intention Data: Progress Report*, Santa Monica, CA: RAND, N-2076-MIL, April 1984.

Orvis, Bruce R., *Relationship of Enlistment Intentions to Enlistment in Active Duty Services*, Santa Monica, CA: RAND, N-2411-FMP, September 1986.

Orvis, Bruce R., and M. T. Gahart, *Relationship of Enlistment Intention and Market Survey Information to Enlistment in Active Duty Military Service*, Santa Monica, CA: RAND, N-2292-MIL, June 1985.

Orvis, Bruce R., and Martin T. Gahart, *Quality-Based Analysis Capability for National Youth Surveys*, Santa Monica, CA: RAND, R-3675-FMP, March 1989.

Orvis, Bruce R., and Martin T. Gahart, with Karl F. Schutz, *Enlistment Among Applicants for Military Service: Determinants and Incentives*, Santa Monica, CA: RAND, R-3359-FMP, January 1990.

Orvis, Bruce R., Michael T. Childress, and J. Michael Polich, *Effect of Personnel Quality on the Performance of Patriot Air Defense System Operators*, Santa Monica, CA: RAND, R-3901-A, 1992.

Orvis, Bruce R., Martin T. Gahart, Alvin K. Ludwig, with Karl F. Schutz, *Validity and Usefulness of Enlistment Intention Information*, Santa Monica, CA: RAND, R-3775-FMP, 1992.

Polich, J. M., James N. Dertouzos, and S. James Press, *The Enlistment Bonus Experiment*, Santa Monica, CA: RAND, R-3353-FMP, April 1986.

Pomazal, Richard J., and James J. Jaccard, "An Informational Approach to Altruistic Behavior," *Journal of Personality and Social Psychology*, Vol. 33, 1976, pp. 317–326.

Research Triangle Institute, *Youth Attitude Tracking Study II, Fall 1983–Fall 1989*, 1984–1990.

Schutz, K. F., *A Practical Guide to MAXLIK*, Santa Monica, CA: RAND, N-1914-RC, October 1983.

Sheppard, B. H., J. Hartwick, and P. R. Warshaw, "The Theory of Reasoned Action: A Meta-Analysis of Past Research with Recommendations for Modifications and Future Research," *Journal of Consumer Research*, Vol. 15, 1988. pp. 325–343.

Smith, D. Alton, Paul Hogan, and Lawrence Goldberg, *Army College Fund Cost-Effectiveness Study*, U.S. Army Recruiting Command, Report SR 90-5, November 1990.

Toomepuu, J., *Costs and Benefits of Quality Soldiers*, Fort Sheridan, IL: U.S. Army Recruiting Command, 1986.

Westat, Inc., *Youth Attitude Tracking Study III, Fall 1990–Fall 1993*, 1991–1994.

Winkler, John D., Judith C. Fernandez, and J. Michael Polich, *Effect of Aptitude on the Performance of Army Communications System Operators*, Santa Monica, CA: RAND, R-4143-A, 1992.